WALK

with

GOD

Let's get social!

 @Publications_International

@PublicationsInternational

www.pilbooks.com

TABLE OF CONTENTS

It can be difficult to keep hope sometimes, to strive to be a beacon of light and positivity when the world around us grows increasingly more detached and desperate. God and his teachings feel more distant now than ever before. We become overwhelmed by the anxieties of our daily lives— our homes, our careers, the health and happiness of our families—as well as the tragedies that befall our neighbors. Take comfort in your faith and look around you with an open heart. When you greet every day with faith, you can find God's love everywhere.

INTRODUCTION

Walk with God is a daily guide to help broaden your devotion as you reflect on the Bible's teachings of peace, harmony, and hope. Throughout this book, you'll find verses, reflections, and prayers for every day of the calendar year. Recognize that although the world may be stricken with conflict, illness, and poverty, God's love prevails in our every warm thought and action. With his words in your heart, you will never walk alone.

WALK WITH GOD

JANUARY

66

Take therefore no thought for the morrow: for the morrow shall take thought for the things of itself. Sufficient unto the day is the evil thereof.

—*MATTHEW 6:34*

LORD, even though I know worry is a useless waste of time and energy, it snares me again and again. Thank you for helping me notice early on that I'm about to wallow in worry once more. As I give this situation to you, Lord, I release my need to worry about it as well. Instead, I look for the blessings in the midst of all that's going on and thank you wholeheartedly for them. I willingly trade my worry for your peace.

66

**For all things are
for your sakes, that
the abundant grace
might through the
thanksgiving of
many redound to the
glory of God.**

—*2 CORINTHIANS 4:15*

AS we learn to trust you, God, we discover
your strengthening presence in various
places and people. Wherever we encounter
shelter, comfort, rest, and peace, we are
bound to hear your voice, welcoming us.
And in whomever we find truth, love,
gentleness, and humility, we are sure to hear
your heartbeat, assuring us that you will
always be near. Thank you, God. Amen.

**And ye now
therefore have
sorrow: but I will
see you again,
and your heart
shall rejoice, and
your joy no man
taketh from you.**
—*JOHN 16:22*

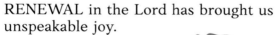

RENEWAL in the Lord has brought us
unspeakable joy.

**Create in me a clean
heart, O God; and
renew a right spirit
within me.**

—PSALM 51:10

LORD, thank you for being a God of new
beginnings. Give me a fresh start today as
I trust in you. Amen.

66

Behold, I make all things new.
—*REVELATION 21:5*

WHEN we think of joy, we often think of things that are new—a new day, a new baby, a new love, a new beginning, the promise of a new home with God in heaven. Rejoicing in these things originates with having joy in the God who makes all things new. Rather than relying on earthly pleasures to provide happiness, the scriptures command that we rejoice in God and in each new day he brings. Joy is a celebration of the heart that goes beyond our circumstances to the very foundation of joy—the knowledge that we are loved by God.

66

**But seek ye first
the kingdom of
God, and his
righteousness; and
all these things
shall be added
unto you.**
—*MATTHEW 6:33*

HOW much happier and at peace would
we be if we allowed God to order our
days? If we just focus on the promises of
his love for us, all else will fall into place
accordingly, without our exhausting effort.

66

That thou wilt do us no hurt, as we have not touched thee, and as we have done unto thee nothing but good, and have sent thee away in peace: thou art now the blessed of the Lord.

—*GENESIS 26:29*

GOD's peace among people brings about many blessings.

66

**For my
brethren and
companions'
sakes, I will
now say, Peace
be within thee.**

—*PSALM 122:8*

SOMETIMES, what we are looking for
exists within us. We love to look outside
of ourselves for peace, joy, and happiness.
But those are gifts of God, and God
empowers us from within. Stop and turn
inward, and there God will be.

> **Be not conformed to this world: but be ye transformed by the renewing of your mind, that ye may prove what is that good, and acceptable, and perfect, will of God.**
>
> —*ROMANS 12:2*

WISE is the soul that cherishes the present without longing for other times. Fortunate is the heart that loves without yearning for what it once had. And blessed is the mind that is at peace with today without regret for the past.

**Thou art my
hiding place; thou
shalt preserve me
from trouble; thou
shalt compass me
about with songs
of deliverance.**

—*PSALM 32:7*

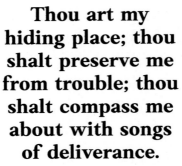

LORD, I need a place to hide. I'm
overwhelmed, with many things to do and
many places to be. Competing demands,
some of which I've put on myself, pull at
me. Help me, Lord. Give me the wisdom
to make good choices. Help me say the
right things. Give me a safe and quiet
place to hide. Give me a moment of peace
and I will sing your praises. Give me a
new song, a song of hope and deliverance.

Great peace have they which love thy law: and nothing shall offend them.

—*PSALM 119:165*

DEAR God,
Your peace is like the sweet calm air after a storm, like a warm blanket on a cold winter day, like a happy smile of someone I love on a day when nothing has gone right. Your peace brings me the comfort and the strength I need to get through the hardest of times and the thickest of situations. I am so grateful, God, for the kind of peace your presence offers me, a peace so deep and abiding I know that no matter what is happening, that peace is there for me to tap into. Like an overflowing well at the center of my being, your presence is the water that quenches my thirst and gives me renewed vigor and life. Thank you, God, for your everlasting peace. Amen.

66

**For he saith to the
snow, Be thou on the
earth; likewise to the
small rain, and to
the great rain of his
strength.**

—*JOB 37:6*

SOMETIMES it is difficult to appreciate
snowy weather, but I thank God for the
gift of snow days. How wonderful it is
for everyone to be home, safe and warm.
On snow days, life returns to a simpler
pace and the demands of schedules and
responsibilities fall away. Thank you, Lord,
for the beauty of the snow and the time
it gives us to relax and share quiet times
with our loved ones.

66

**Fear thou not; for
I am with thee:
be not dismayed;
for I am thy God:
I will strengthen
thee; yea, I will
help thee; yea,
I will uphold
thee with the
right hand of my
righteousness.**

—*ISAIAH 41:10*

TOUCH and soothe my turbulent
emotions, God of still waters. Whisper
words to the listening ears of my soul.
In hearing your voice, give me assurance
beyond a shadow of a doubt that you are
my companion in life, eternally.

66

**Be careful for nothing;
but in every thing by
prayer and supplication
with thanksgiving
let your requests be
made known unto
God. And the peace of
God, which passeth all
understanding, shall keep
your hearts and minds
through Christ Jesus.**

—*PHILIPPIANS 4:6–7*

CALM me enough, O Lord, to breathe
deeply and restoratively despite my racing
heart, pounding headache, and generally
fatigued body and mind. Prayer restores
me in the presence of all that threatens to
undo me, which I name to you now.

66

I exhort therefore, that, first of all, supplications, prayers, intercessions, and giving of thanks, be made for all men; For kings, and for all that are in authority; that we may lead a quiet and peaceable life in all godliness and honesty. For this is good and acceptable in the sight of God our Saviour.

—1 TIMOTHY 2:1–3

YOU, O Lord, are our refuge. When the days are too full and sleep is hard to come by, we simply need to escape to a quiet place and call on you. In your presence we find strength for our work and peace for our troubled minds. We are grateful for the comfort of your embrace, Lord.

66

**He hath shewed thee,
O man, what is good;
and what doth the
Lord require of thee,
but to do justly, and
to love mercy, and to
walk humbly with
thy God?**

—*MICAH 6:8*

STEP by step, I walk towards you, O Lord.
Even though I know the way, sometimes
my steps falter. Please put in my heart the
desire to do good and to walk with you.

> **Trust in the Lord with all thine heart; and lean not unto thine own understanding. In all thy ways acknowledge him, and he shall direct thy paths.**
>
> —*PROVERBS 3:5–6*

GOD, when I feel unsteady, you alone provide the firm ground beneath my feet. Illuminate my path so that I am always living in your will and not from my own limited ego. Show me how to be the best I can be under all circumstances, both good and bad.

66

**Ye are the light of
the world. A city
that is set on an hill
cannot be hid.**

—*MATTHEW 5:14*

SOME people seem to radiate God's light
to others. Their love for God and for
others spills over in everything they do.
I ask your blessing today on those who
work to spread God's light—especially
pastors, teachers, Bible study and prayer
group leaders, and chaplains.

66

**Give to every man
that asketh of
thee; and of him
that taketh away
thy goods ask
them not again.**
—*LUKE 6:30*

WE have been created to love each other,
to help each other, and to heal each
other. In doing so, we love, help, and heal
ourselves.

66

Let us not be weary in well doing: for in due season we shall reap, if we faint not.

—*GALATIANS 6:9*

NANCY's brother Ed has suffered from depression for years. He's on medication now, which helps. And Nancy tries to uplift him (and sometimes succeeds) with daily texts, movie nights together, and the occasional dinner out. "Ed's depression has been a learning experience for me," Nancy shares. "I can be there for him, I can't stop trying, but I cannot expect that every one of my efforts will make a difference. I have to be at peace with that."

Lord, I am discouraged because my efforts to uplift others seem to mean little. Help me to not lose heart. Help me to keep trying.

> **Heal me, O Lord,
> and I shall be healed;
> save me, and I shall
> be saved: for thou art
> my praise.**
> —*JEREMIAH 17:14*

WHEN we pray for healing, we pray for wholeness. Our prayers may be answered even if we don't receive exactly what we thought we asked for: The terminally ill person may be healed, yet not live; the chronically pained may still have physical suffering, yet their healing may mean they have been given an inner peace with which the physical problems are faced.

66

Blessed be God, even the Father of our Lord Jesus Christ, the Father of mercies, and the God of all comfort; Who comforteth us in all our tribulation, that we may be able to comfort them which are in any trouble, by the comfort wherewith we ourselves are comforted of God.

—*2 CORINTHIANS 1:3–4*

LORD, help my eyes to see all the ways you are working in this world. Because of your great compassion, because of your active involvement, the effects of everything you accomplish are multiplied many times over. We praise you, Lord, and pray you will continue to be involved in our lives and in our world. And may our deeds and thoughts always honor you.

66

Study to shew thyself approved unto God, a workman that needeth not to be ashamed, rightly dividing the word of truth.

—*2 TIMOTHY 2:15*

AT work, I manage a team of employees, and it's part of my job to take charge and support those who report to me. Questions? Come to me. Problems? I can help solve them. I take pride in this role, and yet there are times in my own life when I need to remember that I don't have to handle everything. I can—and should—take my problems to God. He actually encourages us to do so because he loves us. Dear Lord, please help me to remember that I can rely on you.

66

Come unto me, all ye that labour and are heavy laden, and I will give you rest. Take my yoke upon you, and learn of me; for I am meek and lowly in heart: and ye shall find rest unto your souls. For my yoke is easy, and my burden is light.

—*MATTHEW 11:28–30*

FATHER God, in you I find comfort and peace after a day of working hard and pushing forward to reach my goals. In you I find strength when I've done all I can do on my own. In you I find my spirit renewed. Amen.

66

They continued stedfastly in the apostles' doctrine and fellowship, and in breaking of bread, and in prayers.

—ACTS 2:42

WHEN I was a child, my mom used to talk about "refilling the well," by which she meant the joy she took in being with people who restored her. I thought of her expression last week when I had lunch with an old classmate; when he and I parted, I was struck by how being with this friend energized rather than depleted me. He is a calm, spiritual person, and our times together never fail to leave me feeling uplifted. Although we don't always agree, we inspire one another to learn and grow. Lord, may I remember the importance of developing relationships with other believers, whose fellowship and spiritual life can help to deepen my faith.

x

66

Fight the good fight of faith, lay hold on eternal life, whereunto thou art also called, and hast professed a good profession before many witnesses.

—*1 TIMOTHY 6:12*

LORD, I do believe! And because of my hope of life with you in eternity, there is all the more meaning for life today. There's meaning in my choices, my relationships, my work, my play, my worship. It all matters, it all counts, and I live knowing one day I'll stand in your presence with great joy.

66

**O Father, glorify
thou me with thine
own self with the
glory which I had
with thee before
the world was.**

—*JOHN 17:5*

ALMIGHTY God, do we tell you often
enough how awesome you are? We
stand before you in complete awe of
your creation, your sovereignty, and
your power. Let us never minimize the
ability you have to change our reality in
an instant, even when it involves moving
mountains or calming storms. You, O God,
are the one and only God, and we give
you glory at all times.

66

**By humility
and the fear
of the Lord
are riches,
and honour,
and life.**

—*PROVERBS 22:4*

THE greatness of God humbles us. That's
because when we are in awe of him, we
think less of ourselves. Then we make
better choices. Then he can open up new
opportunities. Then others can trust us
and respect us. True humility is a new
beginning, an opening to wisdom and
grace. When we see God in his majesty
and glory, we will fear him. Then we find
favor, giving thanks to God.

66

**Neither do men
light a candle,
and put it under
a bushel, but on
a candlestick;
and it giveth light
unto all that are
in the house.**

—*MATTHEW 5:15*

SOMETIMES it is easier to recognize other people's spiritual gifts than our own. Lord, let me be humble, knowing that all good things are from you, but keep me from false humility, where I downplay the genuine spiritual gifts you have given me. Let me not talk myself out of doing your work because I'm afraid I'm not a good enough speaker, or listener, or leader.

"

Faith is the substance of things hoped for, the evidence of things not seen.

—*HEBREWS 11:1*

FAITH is the foundation upon which a happy, healthy life is built. The stronger our faith, the less our life can be shaken by outside occurrences and extraneous circumstances.

"

**Peace I leave
with you, my
peace I give
unto you: not
as the world
giveth, give I
unto you. Let
not your heart
be troubled,
neither let it be
afraid.**

—*JOHN 14:27*

TO live a life of faith is to live always in God's presence, at peace in the home of his love.

WALK WITH GOD

FEBRUARY

Therefore being justified by faith, we have peace with God through our Lord Jesus Christ.

—*ROMANS 5:1*

TO have faith is to have the promise of God's love to see you through any situation in life. Faith accompanies us, helping us to see the next step along the unseen path that is his will. When we step out of faith, we step away from the peace and comfort of God. Walking in faith is walking with God.

66

**I will give peace
in the land, and ye
shall lie down, and
none shall make you
afraid: and I will rid
evil beasts out of the
land, neither shall
the sword go through
your land.**

—LEVITICUS 26:6

TRUE peace comes from the Lord.

❝

Grace be with you, mercy, and peace, from God the Father, and from the Lord Jesus Christ, the Son of the Father, in truth and love.

—2 JOHN 1:3

LORD, make me an instrument of your peace, where there is hatred, let me sow love; where there is injury, pardon; where there is doubt, faith; where there is despair, hope; where there is darkness, light; and where there is sadness, joy.
—St. Francis of Assisi

When a man's ways please the Lord, he maketh even his enemies to be at peace with him.

—PROVERBS 16:7

FATHER, I've noticed that when I make my primary objective to treat people with kindness and respect instead of focusing on our differences, there is a level of respect I receive in return. Even people who might be religious or political "enemies," so to speak, are inclined to permit me my perspectives without being antagonistic toward me. This is not because I water down what I believe in, but because your love can have that effect on people. When your love touches our lives, it subdues animosity and fosters peace. Thank you for showing me how good your command is to love my neighbor as myself. By treating others as I would want to be treated, I can bring some much needed peace into this world.

66

But love ye your enemies, and do good, and lend, hoping for nothing again; and your reward shall be great, and ye shall be the children of the Highest: for he is kind unto the unthankful and to the evil. Be ye therefore merciful, as your Father also is merciful.

—*LUKE 6:35–36*

HEAVENLY Father, give us the forgiving spirit we so badly need to heal the wounds of the past. Help us live "the better life" by making peace with our enemies and understanding that they, too, need your love. Amen.

Be ye kind one to another, tenderhearted, forgiving one another, even as God for Christ's sake hath forgiven you.

—EPHESIANS 4:32

GOD in heaven, teach me to forgive others their transgressions and to let go of angers and resentments that poison the heart and burden the soul. Teach me to love and understand others and to accept them as they are, not as I wish they would be. Amen.

66

Feed the flock of God which is among you, taking the oversight thereof, not by constraint, but willingly; not for filthy lucre, but of a ready mind; Neither as being lords over God's heritage, but being examples to the flock.

—*1 PETER 5:2–3*

LORD, sometimes I find myself upset about minor things. I have an idea in mind about how things should be, and someone else does not cooperate because they have their own preferences for how to do things... help me let go of the need for control. Let me especially have the wisdom to discern when I should be guiding my children, and when I should let them make their own plans and decisions, even when I think I know a better way.

**Lord, thou wilt ordain
peace for us: for thou
also hast wrought all our
works in us.**

—*ISAIAH 26:12*

DEAR God, I long to feel the peace
you bring, the peace that passes all
understanding. Fill my entire being with
the light of your love, your grace, and
your everlasting mercy. Be the soft place
that I might fall upon to find the rest and
renewal I seek. Amen.

For to be carnally minded is death; but to be spiritually minded is life and peace.

—*ROMANS 8:6*

HEAVENLY Father, thank you for the centeredness you bring to my life. Even when every external thing is in an uproar, I can still come back to that still, small place and feel your Holy Spirit. I know you are with me always and that I am your beloved. I can rest in your presence in complete peace, knowing you will protect and shelter me. Thank you for your never-failing love. Amen.

**Keep thy
heart with all
diligence; for
out of it are the
issues of life.**
—*PROVERBS 4:23*

LORD, many times I have asked you to protect my heart from wanton wanderings, and you have always aided me. How grateful I am for your help, Lord. Thank you for steering my heart toward only what is good and true. My heart is full of love for many people, but it only belongs to you.

**My flesh and
my heart
faileth: but God
is the strength
of my heart,
and my portion
for ever.**

—*PSALM 73:26*

LORD, please be my strength. When I am
scared, please make me brave. When I am
unsteady, please bring your stability to me.
I look to your power for an escape from
the pain. I welcome your comfort. Amen.

> **Follow peace
> with all men, and
> holiness, without
> which no man
> shall see the Lord.**
> —*HEBREWS 12:14*

FATHER, you are the greatest of all peacemakers. You made reconciliation with humanity possible by means of great personal sacrifice—but without compromising the truth. Show me how to follow your example today. Help me not to settle for fake peace—the kind that comes when lies are allowed to prevail for the sake of avoiding conflict. Instead, grant me the courage, grace, and wisdom to work toward real peace, which values all people and fulfills our need for truth and love.

**The Lord thy God
in the midst of thee
is mighty; he will
save, he will rejoice
over thee with
joy; he will rest
in his love, he will
joy over thee with
singing.**

—*ZEPHANIAH 3:17*

FATHER, nothing moves me more to love others than reflecting on how you love me. I think of all the things you could have held against me and used as reasons to not love me. And yet you always look for ways to forgive, restore our relationship, and move forward. I want to love like that!

**Beloved, let us
love one another:
for love is of
God; and every
one that loveth is
born of God, and
knoweth God. He
that loveth not
knoweth not God;
for God is love.**

—*1 JOHN 4:7–8*

HEAVENLY Father, you are the author
of love. We are able to love only because
you first loved us. You taught us how
to love you and each other—our family,
our friends, and our neighbors. We want
everyone to know your perfect love, and
we invite the fragrance of your love to
permeate our home.

**Be strong and of
a good courage;
be not afraid,
neither be thou
dismayed: for
the Lord thy
God is with thee
whithersoever
thou goest.**

—JOSHUA 1:9

ALMIGHTY God, today I pray for all those who feel love has passed them by. Due to the circumstances of their lives, they can't think of even one person who truly loves them. How hard it must be to reach out and love others if you have never felt the warmth of love yourself. How that could all change if they come to know you, God! Reach through the loneliness with your love, Father.

**This is my
commandment,
That ye love one
another, as I
have loved you.**

—JOHN 15:12

WHEN I feel alone or lonely, sometimes the best remedy is to do something for someone else—to love God by loving my neighbor! It's so easy to get tangled up in my own isolating concerns. God, please let me seek your Spirit and practice these virtues. Amen.

**But he, willing
to justify
himself, said
unto Jesus,
And who is
my neighbour?**

—*LUKE 10:29*

GOD, there are days when I am perfectly happy to love my neighbor—as long as I get to define who that neighbor is. But when the lawyer asked about his neighbor, you answered with the story of the Good Samaritan. Please help me expand my definition to all those you love, all those you put in my pathway, even when I find that task difficult.

As the Father hath loved me, so have I loved you: continue ye in my love. If ye keep my commandments, ye shall abide in my love; even as I have kept my Father's commandments, and abide in his love.

—*JOHN 15:9–10*

LOVE and obedience are opposite sides of the same coin. If we obey God, we abide in his love. And the Father loves us, just as he loves his own Son. Then, because we love him we obey him, just as the Son obeys the Father. Love and obedience are inseparable. And we are inseparable from God if we abide in him, loving and obeying him. We abide in him because he loves us.

**Surely he
scorneth the
scorners: but
he giveth
grace unto
the lowly.**

—*PROVERBS 3:34*

LORD, I ask that you give me the gift of
humility. Sometimes I get full of myself.
I want to share my faith with a friend,
and instead it turns into something close
to boasting, as if I have it all figured out.
Lord, you are the one who grants me the
grace to walk on this path towards you.
You are the one who draws me back when
I stumble. My best efforts pale next to
your grace.

"

With all lowliness and meekness, with longsuffering, forbearing one another in love; Endeavouring to keep the unity of the Spirit in the bond of peace.

—EPHESIANS 4:2–3

ONE of many things I like about my wife is her ability to laugh at herself. She doesn't take herself too seriously, and because I admire that quality in her, I try as best I can to emulate her humility. Just yesterday, we were talking about my efforts to fix the sink in the bathroom, and when I caught myself becoming defensive, I tried to turn things around by joking. I think my wife was probably relieved to see me making an effort, and so she took up with the joke. Within moments we were both laughing. Things could have gone one way but they took a better turn. Dear Lord, thank you for helping me to remember the importance of humility in a marriage.

Having then gifts differing according to the grace that is given to us, whether prophecy, let us prophesy according to the proportion of faith; Or ministry, let us wait on our ministering: or he that teacheth, on teaching; Or he that exhorteth, on exhortation: he that giveth, let him do it with simplicity; he that ruleth, with diligence; he that sheweth mercy, with cheerfulness.

—*ROMANS 12:6–8*

BLESS our differences, O Lord. And let us love across all barriers, the walls we build of color, culture, and language. Let us turn our eyes upward and remember: The God who made us all lives and breathes and moves within us, untouched by our petty distinctions. Let us love him as he is, for he loves us just as we are.

**The spirit of God
hath made me,
and the breath of
the Almighty hath
given me life.**

—JOB 33:4

WE want to belong and go to great
lengths to fit anonymously in, forgetting
we are like snowflakes, no two, thank God,
alike. Each snowflake and child of yours is
the same in essence but different in form.
Bless our unique, one-of-a-kind value.
We are heartened to know that no one is
created more special. It is not your way to
make one snowflake, or one person, better
than another.

**My soul, wait
thou only upon
God; for my
expectation is
from him.**

—PSALM 62:5

FATHER God, the earth is asleep. The buds of spring lie in wait. The wonder of your world seems in a holding pattern just waiting for the go-ahead to grow. Let winter teach us the value of stillness, of silence, and of meditation. In this time of anticipation, help us do the work of your kingdom of peace.

FEBRUARY 24

66

**I will both lay me
down in peace,
and sleep: for thou,
Lord, only makest
me dwell in safety.**

—*PSALM 4:8*

WE can sleep because God does not. The
reasons we cannot sleep are many. The
reasons we can are few. But the sleep
promised here is because the Lord makes
us "dwell in safety." This assurance that
he watches over us frees us from worry
and fear, providing a rest that is rooted in
Providence.

Sleep itself is a gift, a gracious provision
that allows us to be renewed with fresh
strength and a clear mind. Brought on
by honest labor, it is sweet. And while
we sleep, he works—protecting us and
providing for us even while we rest. What
a wonderful truth.

The sleep of a labouring man is sweet, whether he eat little or much: but the abundance of the rich will not suffer him to sleep.

—*ECCLESIASTES 5:12*

WE toss and turn, God of nighttime peace, making lists of "must do" and "should have done... or not" and wind up feeling unequal to the tasks and sleep-deprived to boot. Bless us with deep sleep and dreams that reveal us as you see us: beloved, worthy, capable. At dawn, help us see possibilities on our lists.

Each time we yawn today, Lord—for it was a short night—we'll breathe in your restorative presence and exhale worries. Tonight we'll sleep like the sheep of your pasture, for we lie down and rise up in your care, restored, renewed, and rested.

Cast thy burden upon the Lord, and he shall sustain thee: he shall never suffer the righteous to be moved.

—*PSALM 55:22*

IT's easy to "borrow trouble," even on days when all seems well. This week was a good one: I met a challenging project deadline and received good feedback on the work I'd done. Our crocuses started blooming, a sure sign that spring is here. And yet, as I poked around the garden, a place that always brings me solace, I found myself worrying about the day when my health might no longer allow me the pleasures I enjoy today. What if my knees give out and I could no longer kneel in my garden to plant and weed? What if some day I don't have the stamina to meet tight work deadlines as I do today? Then my daughter came racing outside to join me. I let myself be in that moment, and in that moment, I felt joy. God, please help me to stay in the here and now.

**Now the Lord
of peace himself
give you peace
always by all
means. The Lord
be with you all.**

—2 THESSALONIANS 3:16

GOD, give me peace of mind today, for I am worried about so many things. Give me peace of heart today, for I am fearful of challenges before me. Give me peace of spirit today, for I am in a state of confusion and chaos. I ask, God, for your peace today, and every day, to help keep my feet on the right path and my faith solid and unmoving. Without peace, I don't see the answers you place before me. Without peace, I cannot hear your still, small voice within. Shower me today with your loving peace, God, and all will be well in my mind, heart and spirit. Amen.

FEBRUARY 28

**He maketh peace
in thy borders,
and filleth thee
with the finest
of the wheat.**

—*PSALM 147:14*

O God, who art the unsearchable abyss
of peace, the ineffable sea of love, the
fountain of blessings, and the bestower of
affection, who sendest peace to those that
receive it; open to us this day the sea of
thy love, and water us with the plenteous
streams from the riches of thy grace.
Make us children of quietness, and heirs
of peace. Enkindle in us the fire of thy
love; sow in us thy fear; strengthen our
weakness by thy power; bind us closely to
thee and to each other in one firm bond of
unity; for the sake of Jesus Christ. Amen.
—Early Liturgical Prayer

Know ye not that ye are the temple of God, and that the Spirit of God dwelleth in you?

—*1 CORINTHIANS 3:16*

LORD, when there seems to be no easy way out of a tough situation, I turn to you. When relationships seem too difficult to navigate, I turn to you. When I fear for my safety or feel threatened by bodily harm, I turn to you. You, O Lord, are my sanctuary. With you I am always safe. I praise you for this night and day!

MARCH

66

Let not mercy and truth forsake thee: bind them about thy neck; write them upon the table of thine heart: So shalt thou find favour and good understanding in the sight of God and man.

—*PROVERBS 3:3–4*

GOD gives us faith as a means of getting in touch with his love. For once we have that love, we can pass it on to others.

66

I will give unto thee the keys of the kingdom of heaven: and whatsoever thou shalt bind on earth shall be bound in heaven: and whatsoever thou shalt loose on earth shall be loosed in heaven.

—*MATTHEW 16:19*

THIS is a promise to the Apostle Peter, after he proclaims his faith in Christ. Jesus says his servant will have the power and authority he needs to do the work God requires. Claim a little bit of that today. In the service of God's kingdom, in the knowledge of his will, you will have the insights and resources you need to do the Father's work. Be bold.

66

This I pray, that your love may abound yet more and more in knowledge and in all judgment; That ye may approve things that are excellent; that ye may be sincere and without offence till the day of Christ.

—PHILIPPIANS 1:9–10

I am here right now, Father, because I do want to walk in your ways. I know the key is staying connected to you because the ways of the world are all around me, always imposing a different set of values and a different worldview. Give me a wise and discerning heart in all things today so I can stay on track.

66

**Let the peace of God
rule in your hearts, to
the which also ye are
called in one body; and
be ye thankful.**

—*COLOSSIANS 3:15*

GOD in heaven, our diversions seem
great. We can't remember when the
insurmountable demands started piling up,
and we have a hard time seeing the end.
Allow us to take a moment from our hectic
days to close our eyes and feel your peace.
We ask you to lead us. Amen.

66

Whosoever drinketh of this water shall thirst again: But whosoever drinketh of the water that I shall give him shall never thirst; but the water that I shall give him shall be in him a well of water springing up into everlasting life.

—*JOHN 4:13–14*

JESUS' peace is here for me. He gave it to those who follow him as an assurance of his abiding presence. Will I choose to give it its place in my soul when troublesome things are jumping out at me or nipping at my heels? God, you have provided a great ocean of peace for my soul.

66

Whither shall I go from thy spirit? or whither shall I flee from thy presence? If I ascend up into heaven, thou art there: if I make my bed in hell, behold, thou art there. If I take the wings of the morning, and dwell in the uttermost parts of the sea; Even there shall thy hand lead me, and thy right hand shall hold me.

—PSALM 139:7–10

THE threat "You can run but you can't hide" gets turned on its head in this passage—transformed into a promise of God's presence with us in all places. The Lord isn't ever going to be left behind when we're in a place that seems distant or unfamiliar. In fact, he's already there. It's a great truth to keep in mind whether we're headed to the dentist today or on a trip around the world.

66

But the salvation of the righteous is of the Lord: he is their strength in the time of trouble.

—PSALM 37:39

SOMETIME today you will fail. Your strength will fail. Your courage will fail. But God will not fail. He will sustain you, encourage you, and help you. No matter what the temptation or trial may be, he is your portion forever, all that you need to take the next step and do the right thing. He is all you need. He is the strength of your heart. He is enough.

Strength and honour are her clothing; and she shall rejoice in time to come.
—*PROVERBS 31:25*

GOD created women as powerful, loving beings. But as women, we get tired and worn out. We burn the candle at both ends. The only way to keep moving forward is to make sure we are healthy, strong, and at peace, so we can then help others.

66

From whence come wars and fightings among you? come they not hence, even of your lusts that war in your members?

—*JAMES 4:1*

SIT with me, God of broken dreams, in the debris of my family. Toddler tantrums, teen rebellion, young-adult resistance. They topple me like a tornado through town even in this time of peacemaking. I'm tempted to finish the destruction with harsh words, yet how can I reject or give up on a child loved by you no matter how much upheaval they cause? Keep me calm.

66

**I wait for the
Lord, my soul
doth wait, and
in his word do
I hope.**

—*PSALM 130:5*

HELP me to slow down, God of patience,
because sometimes I'm so frustrated by
this tough daily grind. I know you have
a plan for me and I see your good works
in my life and those of my loved ones.
But it's hard to keep my mind clear of
negative clutter when I'm in my routine,
caring for my spouse or children, going
to work, feeling stuck. In your Word I
find moments of peace, the promise of
quietude.

66

Which of you shall have a friend, and shall go unto him at midnight, and say unto him, Friend, lend me three loaves; For a friend of mine in his journey is come to me, and I have nothing to set before him? And he from within shall answer and say, Trouble me not: the door is now shut, and my children are with me in bed; I cannot rise and give thee. I say unto you, Though he will not rise and give him, because he is his friend, yet because of his importunity he will rise and give him as many as he needeth.

—*LUKE 11:5–8*

WAITING for your answers to prayer is sometimes excruciating, but I've come to see that these waiting periods are usually good for me. I grow in discipline, and I discover the peace of your presence.

66

**In my distress I called
upon the Lord, and
cried unto my God: he
heard my voice out of
his temple, and my cry
came before him, even
into his ears.**

—*PSALM 18:6*

MY guard is constant and vigilant,
protecting me against the next episode of
my humanness. I know to err is human,
but why does it happen so often? Peace
only comes, God of wholeness, through
reassurance that with you, mistakes,
errors—even disasters—can yield
treasures. I am so grateful.

Then came Peter to him, and said, Lord, how oft shall my brother sin against me, and I forgive him? till seven times? Jesus saith unto him, I say not unto thee, Until seven times: but, Until seventy times seven.

—*MATTHEW 18:21–22*

THANK you, God, for second chances. Sometimes I feel like I can't do anything right. It's embarrassing to make mistakes. It's embarrassing to show others that I am less than perfect. Thank you for giving me the chance to try again, to make things right, and to improve myself. Help me find the courage to try again and show the world my best qualities!

66

Rend your heart, and not your garments, and turn unto the Lord your God: for he is gracious and merciful, slow to anger, and of great kindness, and repenteth him of the evil.

—*JOEL 2:13*

TO show they were sorry, the ancients used to tear their clothes and weep. But the prophet Joel says that's just for show. What God really wants us to do in these times is rend our heart, confessing our sin in contrition and deep sorrow, turning to God, who is gracious and merciful. Then, in his great kindness, he turns away from his anger at what we have done. It's our heart he wants.

> **Finally, brethren, whatsoever things are true, whatsoever things are honest, whatsoever things are just, whatsoever things are pure, whatsoever things are lovely, whatsoever things are of good report; if there be any virtue, and if there be any praise, think on these things.**
>
> —*PHILIPPIANS 4:8*

LORD, I want my thoughts to be like your thoughts. I want to discern what you discern and have the insight you have into all that happens in the world. I know that can never really be, Lord, but if I am open to your Spirit at all times, perhaps I can construe your hopes now and then. May my mind never be so cluttered that I fail to receive a message you are trying to share with me, Lord.

❝

For thus saith the Lord; Like as I have brought all this great evil upon this people, so will I bring upon them all the good that I have promised them.

—*JEREMIAH 32:42*

THE people in Jeremiah's time had made some terrible choices, and they had been punished for them. But God does not forget his promises and will ultimately bring good to his people. You may in fact be suffering the consequences of your actions, but take hope. Find and believe God's promises. A merciful God intends your good.

66

If one prevail against him, two shall withstand him; and a threefold cord is not quickly broken.

—ECCLESIASTES 4:12

MY husband and I don't attend church every Sunday, but each weekend we make time to read scripture and talk about the week, which we try to view through the lens of spirituality. A difficult coworker, good news in our extended families— we'll discuss the good and the bad and talk about how God informs each ebb and flow. Sometimes we'll share a joy, such as the time my husband built a new bird feeder and we both discovered the great calm and pleasure we derived from watching the sparrows and finches. I think we both gain a lot from these quiet, regular moments of sharing. The Bible reminds me how your presence in my life, and my husband's life, creates a powerful "threefold cord." God, if my marriage is grounded in you, it will be strong.

66

His delight is in the law of the Lord; and in his law doth he meditate day and night. And he shall be like a tree planted by the rivers of water, that bringeth forth his fruit in his season; his leaf also shall not wither; and whatsoever he doeth shall prosper.

—*PSALM 1:2–3*

GOD, when my decisions are rooted in your Word, you do not lead me astray. When I am faced with problems and obstacles, let me turn to you and the Bible as I search for solutions, so that I do not act hastily but in accordance with your will.

> **Every good gift and every perfect gift is from above, and cometh down from the Father of lights, with whom is no variableness, neither shadow of turning.**
>
> —*JAMES 1:17*

EVERYTHING around me keeps changing, Lord. Nothing lasts. My relationships with others are different than they were before. I started to feel as if there is nothing sure and steady on which I can depend. Then I remembered your ever-present, unchanging love. Through these transitions, your love gives me courage and hope for the future. Amen.

"

Ask ye of the Lord rain in the time of the latter rain; so the Lord shall make bright clouds, and give them showers of rain, to every one grass in the field.

—*ZECHARIAH 10:1*

I am grateful, God of hope, for the gift of each new day, each new season, like the one unfolding around me now in flower and birdsong, in seedling and bud. When they arrive as surely as dawn follows night and bloom follows bulb, I am uplifted by the fulfillment of your promise.

> **"**
>
> **For the mountains shall depart, and the hills be removed; but my kindness shall not depart from thee, neither shall the covenant of my peace be removed, saith the Lord that hath mercy on thee.**
>
> —*ISAIAH 54:10*

SOME things are predictable. The sun comes up, and the mountain rises majestically above the plain. But even if the mountains fall, his kindness will not depart from you. He will keep his promise of peace with his people, a promise demonstrated and secured by the gift his own Son. This is mercy we do not deserve, but more certain than the hills. This is what the Lord says, and we are glad.

66

Let us therefore follow after the things which make for peace, and things wherewith one may edify another.

—*ROMANS 14:19*

GIVE me the tools for building peace, O God, when tempers flare—inside and outside these four walls. In your wisdom I daily try to impart, needed tools include a kind of heart and faith that measures each tiny rebuilt bridge a triumph.

66

**Forbearing one
another, and
forgiving one
another, if any
man have a
quarrel against
any: even as
Christ forgave
you, so also
do ye.**
—*COLOSSIANS 3:13*

LORD, it's hard to mend a friendship
when trust has been broken. And yet
when we open your Word, we see how
you continued to love your people even
when they abandoned you again and
again! Give us that same ability to love and
forgive in the face of broken trust, Lord.
Heal our relationships as only you can.

66

**For if they fall,
the one will lift
up his fellow: but
woe to him that
is alone when
he falleth; for he
hath not another
to help him up.**

—ECCLESIASTES 4:10

A healthy friendship enhances our lives.
What a blessing to have someone who
wants to share all our joys and sorrows.
We should continually strive to be the
kind of friend God would like us to be—
and the kind of friend that we would like
to have.

"

The kingdom of heaven is like to a grain of mustard seed, which a man took, and sowed in his field: Which indeed is the least of all seeds: but when it is grown, it is the greatest among herbs, and becometh a tree, so that the birds of the air come and lodge in the branches thereof.

—*MATTHEW 13:31–32*

SOMETIMES the smallest gesture can mean so much. I thank you today, Lord, for the smile from a stranger, for the grandchild who wants to share a cookie, for the friend who reached out "just because." I thank you for the colleague who paid a compliment on a new haircut, the spouse who emptied the dishwasher when it was my turn, the teenaged rebel who gave me a hug.

66

We are saved by hope: but hope that is seen is not hope: for what a man seeth, why doth he yet hope for? But if we hope for that we see not, then do we with patience wait for it.

—*ROMANS 8:24–25*

ALMIGHTY God, I know you are supremely faithful! Today I ask you to restore hope to the hopeless. Plant seeds of hope in hearts that have lain fallow for so long. Send down showers of hope on those struggling with illness, persecution, or difficult relationships. Hope that comes from you is hope with the power to sustain us when nothing around us seems the least bit hopeful.

"

**The Lord taketh
pleasure in them
that fear him, in
those that hope in
his mercy.**

—*PSALM 147:11*

LORD, today I pray for all those who
are in desperate need of help in order
to survive: victims of earthquakes and
tornadoes, the homeless, and the physically
and emotionally destitute people of our
world. Make yourself known to them,
Lord. May they all see that their true help
comes only from you! You who created
them will not leave them without help, nor
without hope.

66

**God shall wipe away
all tears from their
eyes; and there shall be
no more death, neither
sorrow, nor crying,
neither shall there be
any more pain: for
the former things are
passed away.**

—*REVELATION 21:4*

LORD, when I see anger and strife
around me, it's difficult to keep my own
equilibrium and trust in you. I try to have
faith, but my faith does falter. When I'm
surrounded by division, let me be rooted
in faith, unshaken by the passing concerns
of this world. Let me be a person of peace
myself—not false peace, that ignores
problems that need to be addressed—but
the true peace that comes from you.

66

The kings of the Gentiles exercise lordship over them; and they that exercise authority upon them are called benefactors. But ye shall not be so: but he that is greatest among you, let him be as the younger; and he that is chief, as he that doth serve.

—*LUKE 22:25–26*

LIVE and let live. It's a great recipe for being at peace with life. I know when I relax and give up playing God, things happen with ease and flow, just as he wills them. His presence gives me the wisdom to stop pushing and forcing and being a control freak. I am not in control anyway, so why not lighten up, let go, and let God? I pray, God, to be calm in mind and patient in spirit. I pray to end the madness and chaos of wanting to control everything, and let you be God instead. I thank you, God, for being the force behind my life.

Let the wicked forsake his way, and the unrighteous man his thoughts: and let him return unto the Lord, and he will have mercy upon him; and to our God, for he will abundantly pardon.

—*ISAIAH 55:7*

I am thankful to the Lord for his gift of forgiveness. I know I am not perfect and I know I make mistakes. Grant me the wisdom and grace to know when I am wrong and to ask for forgiveness. Give me a sense of gratitude toward those who forgive my errors, and help me forgive others who have offended me.

"

Heaviness in the heart of man maketh it stoop: but a good word maketh it glad.

—*PROVERBS 12:25*

WE never know what's going on in the life of another person. The guy who cuts me off in traffic, the checkout clerk who reacts to a query with impatience: the way someone reacts doesn't always reflect how they feel about me; it is often instead a response to the complex circumstances of their life on that given day. God, help me remember to respond to others with grace and kindness—to put good out into the world just for the sake of doing so— for the right words spoken to someone at the right time might lift the worry that burdens another's heart.

WALK WITH GOD

APRIL

> **For I will restore health unto thee, and I will heal thee of thy wounds, saith the Lord.**
> —*JEREMIAH 30:17*

HEAVENLY Father, you say that you will heal me. Please help me realize there are different forms of healing. While your healing is sometimes miraculous and other times almost common and everyday, your healing is on occasion invisible. These are moments when life doesn't seem to change, and I have to look inside to find a place of acceptance. It is in this place where I am reminded that who I am is separate from the pain that invades my life. Please help me to turn my thoughts to you. Amen.

> **I know both how to be abased, and I know how to abound: every where and in all things I am instructed both to be full and to be hungry, both to abound and to suffer need. I can do all things through Christ which strengtheneth me.**
>
> —*PHILIPPIANS 4:12–13*

YOU have made things problematic again, Lord, and I need to see that all this upheaval can be a good thing. Help me, Lord. And thank you for showing me that a thoroughly comfortable existence can rob me of real life.

"

But none of these things move me, neither count I my life dear unto myself, so that I might finish my course with joy, and the ministry, which I have received of the Lord Jesus, to testify the gospel of the grace of God.

—*ACTS 20:24*

WE are products of our environment. I learned from my parents, who learned from their parents, and it is not just what children hear—it is what they see, day in and day out. My parents were good people. I also believe it is my responsibility to live in such a way that carries on their legacy of dignity and grace. I can model that behavior for my own children, teens now, and in so doing inspire them to choose a life informed by Christ's teachings. It is an awesome responsibility to live in such a way that others are inspired to seek the joy of heaven.

> **Therefore I say unto you, Take no thought for your life, what ye shall eat, or what ye shall drink; nor yet for your body, what ye shall put on. Is not the life more than meat, and the body than raiment?**
>
> —*MATTHEW 6:25*

LAST weekend, I was busy washing the car, cutting the grass, and taking my shirts to the dry cleaners. My daughter asked if I might read with her, and I responded that I had a mile-long list of things to do. I thought I was giving my daughter a good lesson in responsibility, but then it occurred to me: were my errands as important as time with my child? There were definitely things I needed to accomplish that day, but I understood that time with my kid was important, too. God, help me to remember that having too many things can be a source of worry. Life is more than material possessions.

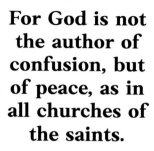

For God is not the author of confusion, but of peace, as in all churches of the saints.

—*1 CORINTHIANS 14:33*

CONFUSION is directing my thoughts. My mind loyally follows its erratic demands and becomes increasingly lost and frustrated. I need a sign to orient myself and to find my way out of this turmoil. Find me, Lord, for I am wandering in the wilderness of my own mind, heading deeper and deeper into despair. Where are you? I call. And then I realize that by describing my lostness, you show me where I am and how to return home.

For nothing is secret, that shall not be made manifest; neither any thing hid, that shall not be known and come abroad.

—*LUKE 8:17*

THERE is great joy when lost things are found—lost lambs, lost coins, but especially lost people. Sometimes we lose our joy, like the older brother in the story of the prodigal son. The good news is that we can turn to God and find it again.

> **The Lord is nigh unto them that are of a broken heart; and saveth such as be of a contrite spirit.**
>
> —*PSALM 34:18*

WHEN grief fills my heart, Father, whether I'm feeling loss, shame, betrayal, or some other sorrow, I know it's temporary, even though at times it feels as though it will never go away. I know that your future for me is joy, and when it comes, I will not reject it. Strengthen me with your joy today, Father. I need it to lift up my soul.

> **We are troubled
> on every side, yet
> not distressed; we
> are perplexed, but
> not in despair;
> Persecuted, but not
> forsaken; cast down,
> but not destroyed.**
> —*2 CORINTHIANS 4:8–9*

DEAR Lord, each night the news is full of trouble. So much pain and sorrow. It makes me ache to see it all. Some nights, it seems that's all there is; this world seems sometimes so weary and heavy laden. Then I turn to you and know that you are nearest on the darkest days. And there is comfort in knowing you and that you have not forsaken us or the people whose world is presently dark. Amen.

> "
>
> **The God of all grace, who hath called us unto his eternal glory by Christ Jesus, after that ye have suffered a while, make you perfect, stablish, strengthen, settle you.**
>
> —*1 PETER 5:10*

WHAT, God of peace, are we to do with our anger? In the wake of trouble, it fills us to overflowing. Sometimes our anger is the only prayer we can bring you. We are relieved and grateful to know that you are sturdy enough to bear all we feel and say. Where do we go from here? What will we be without our anger when it's all that has fueled us? When we are still, we hear your answer: "Emptied." Remind us that, in your redeeming hands, emptiness can become of great use, as a gourd hollowed out becomes a cup or a bowl only when emptied. When the time comes for us to empty ourselves of this abundance of anger, make us into something useful.

In whom we have redemption through his blood, the forgiveness of sins, according to the riches of his grace; Wherein he hath abounded toward us in all wisdom and prudence.

—*EPHESIANS 1:7–8*

LORD, sometimes I fall so low that I feel ashamed and unworthy of being in your presence. At these times, remind me that it is never too late to throw myself at your feet and beg for your forgiveness and mercy. You are all good and all powerful, and your love for us will never waver. I can become whole and joyful again through you.

66

Come, and let us return unto the Lord: for he hath torn, and he will heal us; he hath smitten, and he will bind us up. After two days will he revive us: in the third day he will raise us up, and we shall live in his sight.

—HOSEA 6:1–2

SOME days we deal with the consequences of our failure and sin. The weight is heavy. The pain is real. But these wounds can heal. Even though we have been smitten, he will bind us up. And it won't take long. Even Jesus, dying for all our sins, was only in the grave three days. If you return to the Lord, he will raise you up and you will live in his sight.

66

Blessed are all they that wait for him.

—*ISAIAH 30:18*

THROUGHOUT life, one of the hardest words to hear is "wait." Sometimes we may anxiously wonder, "Where is God when I need him?" And yet we are reminded in scripture that all who wait patiently for him are happy. Patience is developed through faithful waiting. God has a design in even the most difficult situations that will enable our character to become stronger. As we learn patience, we also learn to trust that God has our best interests in mind. He cannot abandon us, and he will always rescue us at just the right time.

He sat down, and called the twelve, and saith unto them, If any man desire to be first, the same shall be last of all, and servant of all.

—MARK 9:35

THOSE who wait patiently for God's direction find inner peace.

66

The Lord bless thee, and keep thee: The Lord make his face shine upon thee, and be gracious unto thee.

—NUMBERS 6:24–25

THE blessing of peace grows best in the soil of faith and wisdom.

66

**It came to pass, as he
sat at meat with them,
he took bread, and
blessed it, and brake,
and gave to them. And
their eyes were opened,
and they knew him; and
he vanished out of
their sight.**

—LUKE 24:30–31

WE don't know how Jesus was changed
in appearance after his resurrection, but
many people did not recognize him at
first. The disciples on the road to Emmaus
recognize him in the breaking of the
bread. Jesus, when we come together to
celebrate the Lord's Supper, let us renew
our faith as we see you again.

66

Have faith in God. For verily I say unto you, That whosoever shall say unto this mountain, Be thou removed, and be thou cast into the sea; and shall not doubt in his heart, but shall believe that those things which he saith shall come to pass; he shall have whatsoever he saith.

—MARK 11:22–23

LORD, how I long to stand strong in the faith! I read of the martyrs of old and question my own loyalty and courage. Would I, if my life depended on it, say, "Yes, I believe in God"? I pray I would, Lord. Continue to prepare me for any opportunity to stand firm for what I know to be true. To live with less conviction is hardly to live at all.

> **They that know
> thy name will
> put their trust
> in thee: for thou,
> Lord, hast not
> forsaken them
> that seek thee.**
>
> —*PSALM 9:10*

LORD, I know you will show your goodness and faithfulness to me if I just diligently seek you. The problem isn't your willingness to give, but my tendency to try to do everything by myself rather than leaning on and trusting in you. This silly inclination brings me needless stress and wastes precious time. Today I endeavor to lay my needs and troubles at your feet the minute I begin to feel the least bit overwhelmed.

APRIL 18

66

**For I will be
merciful to their
unrighteousness,
and their sins and
their iniquities
will I remember
no more.**

—*HEBREWS 8:12*

LORD, today my heart goes out to all those whose past mistakes weigh them down and make any vision they have of their future dreary at best. Oh, that they might know you and the saving grace you bring! Draw near to them today, Lord. Reveal yourself to them in a way that will reach them, and through your mercy and forgiveness, bestow upon them a new vision—a new hope.

> **He said unto Jesus, Lord, remember me when thou comest into thy kingdom. And Jesus said unto him, Verily I say unto thee, Today shalt thou be with me in paradise.**
>
> —*LUKE 23:42–43*

IN extremity, one of the men crucified next to Jesus admitted his wrongdoings and made a connection with Jesus. When I feel like I am too far gone in sin to turn back, and I shouldn't bother with repentance, let me remember this example. It's never too late to seek out Jesus.

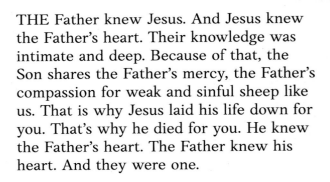

**As the Father knoweth
me, even so know I the
Father: and I lay down
my life for the sheep.**

—*JOHN 10:15*

THE Father knew Jesus. And Jesus knew
the Father's heart. Their knowledge was
intimate and deep. Because of that, the
Son shares the Father's mercy, the Father's
compassion for weak and sinful sheep like
us. That is why Jesus laid his life down for
you. That's why he died for you. He knew
the Father's heart. The Father knew his
heart. And they were one.

**Herein is love,
not that we loved
God, but that he
loved us, and sent
his Son to be the
propitiation for
our sins.**

—1 JOHN 4:10

LORD, we stand in awe of your great
sacrifice for us. Your journey to the cross
is the reason we are free from the
destruction of sin. It's why we can be
forgiven and be united with you throughout
eternity. No sacrifice is too great in
response to your love for us. Keep us ever
mindful, Lord. Keep us ever grateful.

66

We glory in tribulations also: knowing that tribulation worketh patience; And patience, experience; and experience, hope.

—*ROMANS 5:3–4*

GOD, shine your healing light down upon me today, for my path is filled with painful obstacles and my suffering fogs my vision. Clear the challenges from the road I must walk upon, or at least walk with me as I confront them. With you, I know I can endure anything. With you, I know I can make it through to the other side, where joy awaits. Amen.

> **A merry heart
> doeth good like
> a medicine: but
> a broken spirit
> drieth the bones.**
> —*PROVERBS 17:22*

I know you will not fail to lift me up from my sorrow and gently deposit me upon the shore. And though my body is tired and my spirit is weary from weeping, I offer myself to you in complete surrender, so that you may fill my nets with the bounty of your eternal peace and the comfort of your infinite love.

66

Beloved, I wish above all things that thou mayest prosper and be in health, even as thy soul prospereth.

—3 JOHN 1:2

LORD, bless all those today who need healing of any kind. Whether it be physical, emotional, or mental, bless them with your merciful grace and eternal love. Let each one know that they are special in your eyes and that, in the realm of spirit, there is only perfection, wholeness, and joy. Amen.

66

**The Lord, he it is
that doth go before
thee; he will be with
thee, he will not fail
thee, neither forsake
thee: fear not,
neither be dismayed.**

—*DEUTERONOMY 31:8*

THROUGH the darkest days, God walks
beside me and will never leave me. His
presence comforts me and gives me the
courage to keep going no matter what the
circumstances are. Through the darkest
days, God walks beside us.

> **He said unto them, What manner of communications are these that ye have one to another, as ye walk, and are sad?**
>
> —*LUKE 24:17*

JESUS spoke these words to the disciples on the road to Emmaus, when they did not yet recognize him. Sometimes even when we are seeking God, our thoughts seem muddled. We find it difficult to see Jesus present and active in our lives. He seems far away. When we talk to others about our faith, as the disciples spoke to one another, sometimes God's presence becomes clear. How many times, when we look back at confusing times with the benefit of hindsight, do we realize that God was with us!

> **He was seen many days of them which came up with him from Galilee to Jerusalem, who are his witnesses unto the people. And we declare unto you glad tidings, how that the promise which was made unto the fathers, God hath fulfilled the same unto us their children, in that he hath raised up Jesus again.**
>
> —ACTS 13:31–33

IT is good that so many witnesses saw Jesus after the resurrection. It is even better that what they witnessed was the fulfillment of God's promises to Abraham and the prophets. They were promised that all the nations would be blessed by a coming Savior and King. We know it happened because Jesus came back from the dead. That's good news for you. And for everyone.

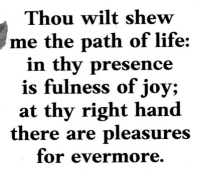

**Thou wilt shew
me the path of life:
in thy presence
is fulness of joy;
at thy right hand
there are pleasures
for evermore.**

—PSALM 16:11

WE all want to be happy, but joy goes much deeper. Joy is not based on circumstances or feelings, which change like the weather. True joy comes from a celebration of the heart over the things that do not change—things that come from God.

"

**Now the God of
hope fill you with
all joy and peace in
believing, that ye
may abound in hope,
through the power
of the Holy Ghost.**

—*ROMANS 15:13*

HOPE, in the biblical sense, is not just
wishing something were true. On the
contrary, we "abound in hope" because
we are joyfully confident that God keeps
his promises. Through the power of the
Holy Spirit, we know his promises are
true. This knowledge fills us with peace
and joy, so lacking in the darkness around
us. Where there is darkness and despair,
we have, and bring, certainty and light.
Our hope is a joyful expectation in the
kindness of our God.

> **Of his fulness have all we received, and grace for grace. For the law was given by Moses, but grace and truth came by Jesus Christ.**
>
> —*JOHN 1:16–17*

YOUR Word and your scriptures give structure to my life. Sometimes I rebel against them, but I know that I am happier and have better relationships with others when I follow the path you have laid out for me.

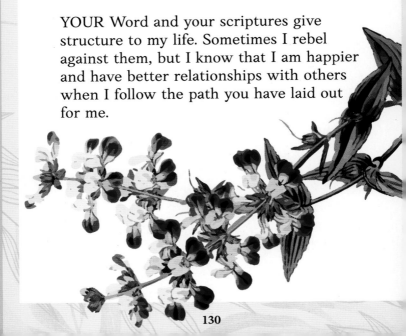

WALK WITH GOD

MAY

66

**Forasmuch then as
Christ hath suffered
for us in the flesh,
arm yourselves
likewise with the
same mind: for he
that hath suffered in
the flesh hath ceased
from sin.**

—*1 PETER 4:1*

DEAR God, no one understands my
suffering, but you do, for you know my
heart even better than I do. Help me to
walk through this dark valley of my pain
and guide me back to the light of truth.
I know that I am precious, but I don't
feel that way right now. Help me see the
reality of who I am—the magnificent
creation you intended me to be. Amen.

**That I may know
him, and the power
of his resurrection,
and the fellowship
of his sufferings,
being made
conformable unto
his death.**

—*PHILIPPIANS 3:10*

THINK of each problem you encounter as nothing more than a challenging reminder from God to think a little higher and reach a little farther. When met with a difficult situation along the road of life, greet it, acknowledge it, and move past it. Then you will be able to continue on your journey a little stronger, a little wiser.

> **My presence shall go with thee, and I will give thee rest.**
> —*EXODUS 33:14*

LORD, we understand that there are and will be problems in our lives, but please remind us of your presence when the problems seem insurmountable. We want to believe that you know best. We hope to remain patient as we search for purpose. Amen.

66

The Lord is my shepherd; I shall not want. He maketh me to lie down in green pastures: he leadeth me beside the still waters. He restoreth my soul: he leadeth me in the paths of righteousness for his name's sake. Yea, though I walk through the valley of the shadow of death, I will fear no evil: for thou art with me; thy rod and thy staff they comfort me.

—*PSALM 23:1–4*

HEAVENLY Father, help us examine every passing day in order to find purpose in our lives. We want our time to be worthwhile. Remind us to count all our blessings, big and small. Amen.

"

I have shewed you
all things, how that
so labouring ye ought
to support the weak,
and to remember the
words of the Lord
Jesus, how he said, It
is more blessed to give
than to receive.

—*ACTS 20:35*

SOW generosity and love; reap unity and peace.

> He that hath pity upon
> the poor lendeth unto
> the Lord; and that
> which he hath given
> will he pay him again.

—PROVERBS 19:17

A generosity motivated by compassion does not go unnoticed. It is always repaid. However, it is not the person to whom we gave who repays us. It is the Lord himself. This frees us from having self-focused expectations or making unreasonable demands. The Lord makes himself our debtor. All that's required of us is our compassion.

"

Charity suffereth long, and is kind; charity envieth not; charity vaunteth not itself, is not puffed up, Doth not behave itself unseemly, seeketh not her own, is not easily provoked, thinketh no evil; Rejoiceth not in iniquity, but rejoiceth in the truth; Beareth all things, believeth all things, hopeth all things, endureth all things.

—*1 CORINTHIANS 13:4–7*

WHEN I think about your example of love, dear God, I realize that love is far more than a warm emotion. It is a deep commitment to look out for another's best interest, even at my own expense. Please teach me to put my pride and my heart on the line. Please protect me, Lord, as I love others in your name. Amen.

66

**Eli answered and said,
Go in peace: and the God
of Israel grant thee thy
petition that thou hast asked
of him. And she said, Let
thine handmaid find grace
in thy sight. So the woman
went her way, and did eat,
and her countenance was no
more sad.**

—*1 SAMUEL 1:17–18*

WHEN Hannah, who is barren, comes
to the temple to pray for a child, Eli the
priest assures her that God has heard her
tearful and anguished prayer. With this
assurance, her face lightens and she is "no
more sad." Whatever emptiness you feel,
may you find joy today in the assurance of
God's grace. He hears your prayer, too. Go
your way, eat, and be glad.

For thou hast possessed my reins: thou hast covered me in my mother's womb.

—*PSALM 139:13*

I offer up prayers today for all expectant parents. Keep mother and child healthy. Ease any anxieties to make this a time of anticipation instead of fear. What promise new life brings!

> **Ye call me Master and Lord: and ye say well; for so I am. If I then, your Lord and Master, have washed your feet; ye also ought to wash one another's feet.**
>
> —*JOHN 13:13–14*

AS a parent of two little girls, I am deeply aware of how my children learn—not just from what I say, but what I do. Jesus set the example of service, and I try to set a good example of service for my children's sake. Every week, I take the kids to volunteer at a local animal shelter. I think it's good for my daughters to see an adult cheerfully and voluntarily offering time and effort to a cause. "It feels good to do something good, doesn't it?" my daughter said the other day. I feel happy for her that she's coming to that realization at a relatively young age. God, thank you for my children. Thank you for helping me to teach them to put good out into the world.

66

What is thy mother? A lioness: she lay down among lions, she nourished her whelps among young lions.

—EZEKIEL 19:2

LORD, you know a mother's heart. You know the panic in the middle of the night when the fever won't go down. You know the butterflies in the stomach when the school bus pulls up to the curb, and a little one heads off to kindergarten. Bless all mothers, Lord. Give them your wisdom and encouragement throughout their busy day, and when the day is over, give them peace and blessed rest.

66

The fear of the Lord is the beginning of wisdom: and the knowledge of the holy is understanding. For by me thy days shall be multiplied, and the years of thy life shall be increased. If thou be wise, thou shalt be wise for thyself: but if thou scornest, thou alone shalt bear it.

—*PROVERBS 9:10–12*

WISDOM begins with the awe of God and ends with understanding ourselves. That's because through him we have a long life, a life with wisdom, confidence, and hope instead of scorn and self-doubt. To fear the Lord is to be in awe of his majesty and mercy. Pause and contemplate his complete goodness and boundless grace. See yourself as the object of his love.

**The Lord our God
be with us, as
he was with our
fathers: let him
not leave us, nor
forsake us.**

—*1 KINGS 8:57*

LORD, on days when everything seems to go wrong, help me to remember that you are always nearby to offer comfort. It is easy to get overwhelmed and feel lost and alone in this world, but deep down I know that is never the case. You are always at the ready to help—I just need to remember to take a moment to stop, breathe, and pray.

Humble yourselves therefore under the mighty hand of God, that he may exalt you in due time: Casting all your care upon him; for he careth for you.

—*1 PETER 5:6–7*

WE would always like to worry a little, enough to make us feel like we can manage on our own. We can't. That's why Peter tells us to cast all our care on God, who cares for us. It takes humility to do this, to depend on his mighty hand completely. Just a little self-sufficiency would be nice. But then it would also be insufficient. Better to trust him with our cares because he cares for us, and exalts us in due time.

> I have called upon
> thee, for thou wilt
> hear me, O God:
> incline thine ear
> unto me, and hear
> my speech.
>
> —*PSALM 17:6*

LORD, I pray I can find a place within my heart where I can let go of worries. I want to be filled with the calmness of a faith in you. Amen.

**In the multitude
of my thoughts
within me thy
comforts delight
my soul.**

—*PSALM 94:19*

DROP thy still dews of quietness,
Till all our strivings cease;
Take from our souls the strain and stress,
And let our ordered lives confess
The beauty of thy peace.
—J. G. Whittier

"

**I know all the fowls
of the mountains: and
the wild beasts of the
field are mine.**

—*PSALM 50:11*

IN my attempts to "get it right" as I order
my life and the lives of those in my family,
remind me, O Creator God, to look around
and see how you have brought order to
our world. Such balance, such harmony,
such stability. May I find the faith to trust
you like a bird trusts the winds that allow
it to soar.

> **But the fruit of the Spirit is love, joy, peace, longsuffering, gentleness, goodness, faith, meekness, temperance: against such there is no law.**
> —*GALATIANS 5:22–23*

LORD, please help me to remember that you are the source of all good things that come out of my life as I grow and flourish in you. All the "good fruit" of love, joy, peace, patience, kindness, goodness, faithfulness, gentleness, and self-control come directly from you and then produce good things in me. I want to thank you for nourishing and supporting my life. Please use the fruit you're producing in me to nourish others and to lead them to you as well.

> **He will not suffer thy foot to be moved: he that keepeth thee will not slumber. Behold, he that keepeth Israel shall neither slumber nor sleep.**
>
> —*PSALM 121:3–4*

HAVE courage for the great sorrows of life and patience for the small ones; and when you have laboriously accomplished your daily task, go to sleep in peace. God is awake.
—Victor Hugo

> **It is vain for you to rise up early, to sit up late, to eat the bread of sorrows: for so he giveth his beloved sleep.**
>
> —*PSALM 127:2*

LORD, why is it that when I am the most tired or crave sleep myself, the children's bedtime becomes prolonged and difficult? There is always one last drink of water, one final trip to the bathroom, one more bedtime story, or one more postscript to the prayer. By then, desperation sets in, and my temper becomes short.

God of peace, help me to face bedtime more calmly. Help me to discover strategies for helping my children to wind down and relax. Prevent me from losing my temper, and grant me a soothing manner so the children's last memories of the day are pleasant and loving. Thank you, Lord, for your promise of a safe and peaceful sleep.

"

And to esteem them very highly in love for their work's sake. And be at peace among yourselves. Now we exhort you, brethren, warn them that are unruly, comfort the feebleminded, support the weak, be patient toward all men.

—*1 THESSALONIANS 5:13–14*

LORD, how grateful we are for the rest you bring to even the most harried souls. The young soldier on the battlefield knows that peace, and so does the young mother with many mouths to feed but too little money in her bank account. You are the one who brings us to the place of restoration in our hearts and minds, Lord. Thank you for being our shepherd.

**We love him,
because he
first loved us.**

—1 JOHN 4:19

DEAR God, thank you for children who teach us to be open and forgiving. Help us forgive those who hurt us so the pain will not be passed on through the generations. Thank you for forgiving our sins and help us be at peace with our families. Amen.

66

The sacrifices of God are a broken spirit: a broken and a contrite heart, O God, thou wilt not despise.

—*PSALM 51:17*

HEAVENLY Father, when I was young, I thought all things hurt or broken could be fixed: knees, feelings, bicycles, tea sets. Now I've learned that not everything can be repaired, relived, or cured. As a mother comforts her child, heal my hurting and grant me the peace I used to know. This I pray. Amen.

66

The heart of the prudent getteth knowledge; and the ear of the wise seeketh knowledge.

—PROVERBS 18:15

I ask your blessing on all students today, as they wrap up their semester, taking finals and finalizing projects. Please keep safe in their travels all those college students coming home, and help them have a good leave. It can be tricky for families to navigate old patterns and new changes.

> **The glory of
> young men is their
> strength: and the
> beauty of old men
> is the grey head.**
>
> —*PROVERBS 20:29*

LORD, how I pray for the young people I love as they head out into the world on their own. Help them tune in to your presence, Lord, and make them wise beyond their years. Warn them of dangers and protect them from the schemes of others. Teach them to love themselves and others extravagantly, but wisely as well. They are your children, Lord, and you love them even more than I do. I place them in your hands.

For the Son of God, Jesus Christ, who was preached among you by us, even by me and Silvanus and Timotheus, was not yea and nay, but in him was yea. For all the promises of God in him are yea, and in him Amen, unto the glory of God by us.

—*2 CORINTHIANS 1:19–20*

WHEN it comes to God's promises, Jesus is all yes. Yes, that's true. Yes, that matters. Yes, that will happen. Amen. So be it. No wavering with Jesus, no nay-saying or doubt. His words and acts reveal God's promises are absolutely true and sufficient. For this we can and should praise God— and even preach a little when we have a chance.

"

**I will sacrifice unto
thee with the voice of
thanksgiving; I will
pay that that I have
vowed. Salvation is of
the Lord.**

—*JONAH 2:9*

ISN'T it funny how we make promises to
God in prayer when we want something?
"God, do this for me and I promise I will..."
I know I do, and I don't always keep those
promises. But God always keeps his vows
to me, and for that I am eternally grateful.
Thanks be to a God that never betrays his
Word. Thanks be to a God that asks us
for sacrifices, but knows that we will be
repaid with his grace. Thanks be to a God
that demands our faith and nothing more,
but rewards us with his eternal presence
and unceasing love. I know in my heart
that when God makes me a promise, he
will keep it forever.

66

**I say unto you, Love
your enemies, bless
them that curse you, do
good to them that hate
you, and pray for them
which despitefully use
you, and persecute you.**

—*MATTHEW 5:44*

WHETHER we keep an actual prayer
list, a list in our heads, or no list at all,
it is good to keep others in our prayers.
We have the privilege of being able to
pray for our family members, and what
a relief it is to be able to entrust them to
God's care when we feel disheartened or
overwhelmed. Jesus even told us to pray
for our enemies! There isn't a soul on the
face of the earth who doesn't need prayer,
who doesn't need God's intervention in
their lives. And who knows? Perhaps
someone is praying for you, too—right at
this very moment.

66

The Lord is nigh unto all them that call upon him, to all that call upon him in truth.

—PSALM 145:18

GOD, it's a quiet day. Help me pause to listen to you, to talk to you, to enjoy your company. Chase away my guilt and shame and fear, and draw me close to your heart. Remind me that no matter what my earthly roles may be, in your presence I am your child, and you care for me more than I could ever imagine. Let me lean against your heart now, Father, and hear it beating with love for me. Amen.

" "

**Hope maketh not
ashamed; because the
love of God is shed
abroad in our hearts
by the Holy Ghost
which is given unto us.**
—ROMANS 5:5

OUR confidence, even our boldness,
comes from the love of God. By his
Spirit, his love simply shines in our lives
and encourages others. How can we be
ashamed of it? How can we hide it?
There is nothing more precious. And there
is nothing more true. This is our great
expectation and hope: We are loved by the
creator and ruler of the universe who gave
us his Spirit. That makes today, and every
day, a good day.

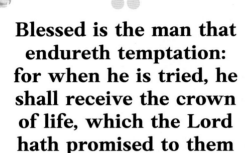

Blessed is the man that endureth temptation: for when he is tried, he shall receive the crown of life, which the Lord hath promised to them that love him.

—*JAMES 1:12*

GOD of the strong and the weak, the brave and the fearful, I come before you to place myself in your loving hands. Take my broken places and make them whole. Heal my wounds that I might be strong for you. Give me patience to accept your timing, And help me to trust in your goodness. In your gracious name, I pray. Amen.

WALK WITH GOD

JUNE

66

When thou passest through the waters, I will be with thee; and through the rivers, they shall not overflow thee: when thou walkest through the fire, thou shalt not be burned; neither shall the flame kindle upon thee.

—*ISAIAH 43:2*

GOD's presence is your promise, even in a flood of fear, doubt, grief, or discouragement. He will be with you. There is comfort in that. And more than that, these things will not overwhelm you because they will not overwhelm him. Floods rise. Floods recede. But God will be with you always.

66

**They that wait upon
the Lord shall renew
their strength; they shall
mount up with wings as
eagles; they shall run, and
not be weary; and they
shall walk, and not faint.**

—*ISAIAH 40:31*

EVEN the young "shall faint and be
weary" (verse 30). But those who wait
on the Lord renew their strength. This is
the strength we want, the strength to run
to him for whom we wait, the one who
delivers us and renews us every day.

66

For which of you, intending to build a tower, sitteth not down first, and counteth the cost, whether he have sufficient to finish it?

—LUKE 14:28

THE first step toward accomplishing any goal is to make a plan. Ask God to help you lay the blueprint for your dream, for he knows best the right tools to use, and the strongest materials to build with.

"

If ye suffer for righteousness' sake, happy are ye: and be not afraid of their terror, neither be troubled.

—*1 PETER 3:14*

EVERYTHING in my life lately seems to be going wrong. People are uncaring. Things I've worked hard for don't seem to be coming to fruition. Everyone needs my time and attention and I feel so tired and overwhelmed and stressed. I ask today in prayer for peace, for serenity. I don't ask for a removal of my problems, but for the power and fortitude to deal with them as they arise from a place of calm and stillness within. I know that you can provide me that kind of amazing, unerring peace, God. Be the rock upon which I can take comfort and rest when the world spins out of control all around me. Be my peace everlasting, dear God. Amen.

66

**The discretion of a
man deferreth his
anger; and it is his
glory to pass over a
transgression.**

—*PROVERBS 19:11*

⸺⸺⸺⸺⸺⸺⸺⸺⸺⸺⸺⸺⸺⸺⸺⸺⸺⸺⸺⸺⸺

LORD above, you look down upon us,
and still you love us. When we look down
on others, it is because we are angered
and cannot see their points of view. We
also still love them, but sometimes our
anger clouds our love. Please help us stay
grounded and find understanding. Amen.

> **He that covereth his sins shall not prosper: but whoso confesseth and forsaketh them shall have mercy.**
>
> —*PROVERBS 28:13*

LORD, teach me to think ahead about the results my actions might inflict. If things go awry despite my forethought, help me admit my wrongs and right them. Amen.

For if ye forgive men their trespasses, your heavenly Father will also forgive you: But if ye forgive not men their trespasses, neither will your Father forgive your trespasses.

—*MATTHEW 6:14–15*

FORGIVENESS is the first step to spiritual freedom. We cannot truly pray with an open heart if we are filled with malice toward ourselves or others.

> **Lo, children are an heritage of the Lord: and the fruit of the womb is his reward. As arrows are in the hand of a mighty man; so are children of the youth.**
>
> —PSALM 127:3–4

I want to pray for the children in my life, Father. They're so innocent, and this world can sometimes be a harsh place. Thank you for assigning them a special place in your care and for giving their guardian angels direct access to you at all times. Be with them today, protect them—heart, soul, mind, and body. I know they will thrive in your love.

For if a man know not how to rule his own house, how shall he take care of the church of God?

—*1 TIMOTHY 3:5*

THOUGH we may not choose our family members we eventually come to the understanding that someone far wiser chose them for us. Each family member has something special to teach us, whether it be forgiveness, tolerance, or acceptance. Some members give us nothing but love. Some give us nothing but grief. It is the former we often embrace, yet it is the latter from which we have the most to learn.

66

But to do good and to communicate forget not: for with such sacrifices God is well pleased.

—HEBREWS 13:16

SHARING has to be one of life's most difficult lessons—for the kids, for me, for everyone, O Bountiful God. Remind me that to choose to give away my time, my energy, myself, makes a gracious gift instead of a grudging duty.

> **Better it is to be of an humble spirit with the lowly, than to divide the spoil with the proud.**
>
> —*PROVERBS 16:19*

SO much need around us, O Lord. Inspire me to teach the children how to care for those who need. Even the smallest gesture in the hand of a child is more powerful than magic, bringing moments of peace and contentment into circumstances thought hopeless. Help me to become childlike in my care for others.

66

They that be wise shall shine as the brightness of the firmament; and they that turn many to righteousness as the stars for ever and ever.

—*DANIEL 12:3*

LORD, let my light shine today, as Jesus taught: "Let your light so shine before men, that they may see your good works, and glorify your Father which is in heaven" (Matthew 5:16). Let my life today reflect your glory because such wisdom is very, very bright. It is so bright, it helps me see clearly. And it is so bright it helps others see, too. It turns many to righteousness, and your kingdom grows, day by day.

66

Delight thyself also in the Lord: and he shall give thee the desires of thine heart.

—*PSALM 37:4*

WHAT a wonderful promise. The Lord will give you the desires of your heart. There is that small catch, however. First you have to delight yourself in the Lord. In fact, the preceding verse adds even more to the expectations: "Trust in the Lord, and do good; so shalt thou dwell in the land, and verily thou shalt be fed." Believers across history have found the secret to this promise. As we delight in him our desires change. Our greatest desire becomes him. We find that "he hath prepared for them a city" (Hebrews 11:16). Other desires change too. We find that our desire is to help others or to change our attitudes. This is what he gives to those who seek him.

JUNE 14

The just man walketh in his integrity: his children are blessed after him.

—*PROVERBS 20:7*

ONE way or the other, children carry the reputation and even the habits of their parents. This proverb reminds us that it can be a blessing for them rather than a curse. Our children will be blessed and helped by people who trusted us. They may squander this blessing, of course. But our integrity is a good place for them to start. That's a good thing for us to remember.

66

He arose, and came to his father. But when he was yet a great way off, his father saw him, and had compassion, and ran, and fell on his neck, and kissed him.

—*LUKE 15:20*

MY heart is full of gratitude, O God, when I think of my husband and the miraculous way you brought us together. I realize now it was you who chose him to be the father of my children.

He is a man of integrity and worth, generous and loving, with the ability to laugh at himself: a perfect combination for a parent.

His loyalty and faithfulness are unquestioned. I am proud to be his wife and prouder still to have my children call him Dad. I humbly thank you, Lord, for this uncommon blessing you have given to me and our children: a faithful man and a man of faith.

"

For every one that asketh receiveth; and he that seeketh findeth; and to him that knocketh it shall be opened. If a son shall ask bread of any of you that is a father, will he give him a stone? or if he ask a fish, will he for a fish give him a serpent?

—*LUKE 11:10–11*

WHEN I want something badly, I don't see all the potential downsides to having it. Father God, please let me ask for those things that are in line with your will for me. Most especially let me ask for the guidance and wisdom of your Holy Spirit in my life.

"

**Pleasant words are
as an honeycomb,
sweet to the soul, and
health to the bones.**

—*PROVERBS 16:24*

YESTERDAY when I was talking with a
friend, she said exactly the thing I needed
to hear, at exactly the time when I needed
to hear it, phrased exactly the right way.
I believe you were working through her
yesterday! When she was willing to be
open to the promptings of the Spirit, and I
was willing to listen, you blessed us with a
special moment where we could see your
love at work.

66

Not only they, but ourselves also, which have the firstfruits of the Spirit, even we ourselves groan within ourselves, waiting for the adoption, to wit, the redemption of our body.

—ROMANS 8:23

IF you want your dreams to bear big fruit, you must be patient enough to let the buds grow into fullness, even if it feels like it's taking forever. Remember, God's timing is not your timing. Stick to it! Don't give up just before you get that bold breakthrough!

66

Wealth gotten by vanity shall be diminished: but he that gathereth by labour shall increase.

—*PROVERBS 13:11*

GOD rewards hard work. It is profitable, both financially and spiritually. We earn and we learn. So set your mind to it, and your back if necessary. Little by little you will gather more. However, work that is useless or empty brings less and less. Do your work well today, humbly open to the possibilities of God's grace, and expect an increase.

**My soul melteth
for heaviness:
strengthen thou
me according
unto thy word.**
—*PSALM 119:28*

GOD Almighty, please help me to put everything into perspective. I want to be realistic but also optimistic. Please send me hope and give me strength of mind to make things right again. Amen.

66

There is one glory of the sun, and another glory of the moon, and another glory of the stars: for one star differeth from another star in glory.

—*1 CORINTHIANS 15:41*

LORD, it's so easy for us to get bogged down in the details of life on this earth. But when we have the opportunity to gaze up at the stars on a clear night, it is easy to remember that there is so much more to your creation than our relatively insignificant lives. You placed the stars and know them by name, Lord, and you know us by name too. We are blessed to be even a tiny part of your magnificent creation! That you also care so deeply for us is the best gift of all.

66

This is the day which the Lord hath made; we will rejoice and be glad in it.

—PSALM 118:24

EARLIER this week I took it upon myself to visit a local botanic garden. I went on a weekday this time, which meant that the park was much less crowded. I appreciated the solitude, and chose to walk a path that winds around a small lake and through pinewoods. The path is made of wood chips, and as I rounded a bend, I heard a crunching noise. Imagine my surprise when I found myself face to face with a deer! The doe looked at me with clear brown eyes, unafraid, and I tried to remain perfectly still. I do not think I exaggerate when I say that we shared a moment; then she regained herself and bounded away. I am so glad I made the effort to visit the botanic garden that day! Dear Lord, thank you for an encounter that filled my spirit.

> **The Lord lift up his countenance upon thee, and give thee peace.**
>
> —*NUMBERS 6:26*

WALKING through the neighborhood on a sunny day, I exchanged smiles with an elderly couple doing the same. Thank you for this moment of shared joy. Sometimes your gifts are big ones. Sometimes they're small and simple: a sunny day, the rustling of the trees, a smile from a stranger, a sense of peace.

"

**Train up a child
in the way he
should go: and
when he is old,
he will not
depart from it.**

—*PROVERBS 22:6*

SEEING my children grow more independent is tremendously rewarding, but sometimes it brings a bit of sadness too, as they naturally spend more time with their friends and studies and hobbies. Father, please give me a generous and encouraging heart. Let me support their independence even as I provide a safe haven for them to return to when they run into problems and need some advice or just a listening ear.

66

For by grace are ye saved through faith; and that not of yourselves: it is the gift of God: Not of works, lest any man should boast. For we are his workmanship, created in Christ Jesus unto good works, which God hath before ordained that we should walk in them.

—*EPHESIANS 2:8–10*

ALTHOUGH our eyes should always be turned above toward God, sometimes we can do with a reminder of God's work just a little bit closer to home. The faith of others can serve as a reminder or an inspiration to strengthen our own faith. Just as we should provide encouragement to others, we can draw on others to help steady ourselves.

66

**Abide in me, and
I in you. As the
branch cannot
bear fruit of itself,
except it abide in
the vine; no more
can ye, except ye
abide in me.**

—*JOHN 15:4*

YOU can find no safer place than abiding
in Jesus. You can find no more fruitful
place either. He is the vine, the source of
our nourishment and strength. Are you
firmly attached to him today? If so, you
can be a blessing to many others, bearing
the fruit of his righteousness and peace—
but only if you abide in him, and let him
abide in you.

He hath made every thing beautiful in his time: also he hath set the world in their heart, so that no man can find out the work that God maketh from the beginning to the end.

—*ECCLESIASTES 3:11*

LORD, how awesome you are, and how incredible your works. Every time I go hiking, I see something just a little bit different. No sunset or sunrise is the same. You continue your work of joyful creation every day!

66

Set your affection on things above, not on things on the earth.

—COLOSSIANS 3:2

I admit that the slightest distraction can pull my mind out of its orbit around you, Father. You know how I am: I can be praying or praising you one minute, and the next moment a phone call with some disturbing news or a careless driver cuts me off and POOF!—my peace has left the building, and I'm all out of sorts. I want to ask you, though, to help me. I want to grow into a more steadfast frame of mind—one that can take bad news and thoughtless people in stride, acknowledging them for what they are, but not allowing them to rattle my world. Would you help me take a step in that direction today? Thank you, Father.

**Who shall separate
us from the
love of Christ?
shall tribulation,
or distress, or
persecution,
or famine, or
nakedness, or peril,
or sword?**

—*ROMANS 8:35*

TURMOIL is the opposite of peace. We
can achieve inner peace by acknowledging
our turmoil, then shifting our focus toward
the healing we desire.

66

For our light affliction, which is but for a moment, worketh for us a far more exceeding and eternal weight of glory.

—*2 CORINTHIANS 4:17*

MAY you be healed, in mind, body, and soul. May you come to know that all healing proceeds from God, and he cares about every part of you. Perhaps the healing will come sooner for your attitude than for your body. Perhaps your mind will experience peace quicker than bones and muscles. But sooner or later, all will be well.

WALK WITH GOD

JULY

66

As we have therefore opportunity, let us do good unto all men, especially unto them who are of the household of faith.

—*GALATIANS 6:10*

O Lord, we give thanks for your presence, which greets us each day in the guise of a friend, a work of nature, or a story from a stranger. We are reminded through these messengers in our times of deepest need that you are indeed watching over us. Lord, we have known you in the love and care of a friend, who envelopes and keeps us company in our despair. When we observe the last morning glory stretching faithfully to receive warmth from your sunshine, we are heartened and inspired to do the same. When we are hesitant to speak up and then read in the newspaper a story of courage, we find our voice lifted and strengthened by your message in black-and-white type. Lord, we are grateful receivers of all the angelic messages that surround us every day.

He that hath my commandments, and keepeth them, he it is that loveth me: and he that loveth me shall be loved of my Father, and I will love him, and will manifest myself to him.

—JOHN 14:21

IF God has touched us with his love, the result will be love flowing through us to others. When we realize the depth of his love, our hearts long to show that kind of love to those around us.

He taught, saying unto them, Is it not written, My house shall be called of all nations the house of prayer? but ye have made it a den of thieves.

—MARK 11:17

WE all prefer to deal with honest people—people we can trust—people who will not lie or try to deceive us. A noble goal for one's life is to pursue honesty— honesty with others, with ourselves, and with God. Yet it is not natural to tell the truth. Honesty can seem to leave us open to attack—to tear down the walls of protection we would rather erect in our lives. Scripture tells us, "The truth shall make you free." Although it might be hard to be honest, if we do it with loving intentions, the burden that dishonesty brings will be lifted.

"

If the Son therefore shall make you free, ye shall be free indeed.

—*JOHN 8:36*

THE freedom Christ gives is not the freedom to do what we want, but the freedom to do what we should. It is, after all, the truth he brings that sets us free. The truth of his Word and the presence of his Spirit give us both wisdom and strength, freeing us from the bondage of our selfishness and pride. The freedom he gives is true freedom, because if the Son makes us free, we are free indeed.

66

For I know the thoughts that I think toward you, saith the Lord, thoughts of peace, and not of evil, to give you an expected end. Then shall ye call upon me, and ye shall go and pray unto me, and I will hearken unto you.

—*JEREMIAH 29:11–12*

THE Lord's plans take time. Here God promises Israelites exiled in Babylon that he will bring them home. They really want to come home. But he isn't in a hurry. In verse 10 he says, "After seventy years be accomplished at Babylon I will visit you, and perform my good word toward you, in causing you to return to this place." In the meantime, he says, settle down, plant gardens, and marry off your kids (verses 4–6). "And seek the peace of the city whither I have caused you to be carried away captives" (verse 7). He has promised us a future. What will we do while we wait for it?

And the very God of peace sanctify you wholly; and I pray God your whole spirit and soul and body be preserved blameless unto the coming of our Lord Jesus Christ.

—1 THESSALONIANS 5:23

ABIDE, O dear Redeemer,
Among us with thy Word
And thus now and hereafter
True peace and joy afford. Amen.
—Traditional prayer

Now the Lord my God hath given me rest on every side, so that there is neither adversary nor evil occurrent.

—*1 KINGS 5:4*

I run my own business, and while I appreciate the many perks of my lifestyle—working from home, a flexible schedule, being my own boss—I sometimes find myself burning the midnight oil. The other night I was awake well into the early hours of the morning. Those dark hours can be lonely ones. As I wrapped up for the night and put my calculator aside, I felt worn out—not just physically, but emotionally. But as I made my way up the stairs to bed, I thought about Christ's promise of giving rest to the weary, and I was comforted. "I'm too tired to do anything more," I thought and, giving over the day's work to Jesus, slept well. God, thank you for the gift of your son, who is there for us to share our burden and restore us with rest.

66

**My brethren, count
it all joy when ye fall
into divers temptations;
Knowing this, that the
trying of your faith
worketh patience. But
let patience have her
perfect work, that ye
may be perfect and
entire, wanting nothing.**

—*JAMES 1:2–4*

FATHER, make me resilient like the sandy
beach upon which the waves crash. Make
me strong like the mighty willow tree
that bends but does not break in the high
winds. Give me the patience and wisdom
to know that my suffering will one day
turn to a greater understanding of your
ways, your works, and your wonders.

There he found a certain man named Aeneas, which had kept his bed eight years, and was sick of the palsy. And Peter said unto him, Aeneas, Jesus Christ maketh thee whole: arise, and make thy bed. And he arose immediately.

—*ACTS 9:33–34*

LOVING Jesus, healer of the sick, I place in your hands myself and all who need your healing. Help us crave the healing that only you can give. May we not define what that healing should be, but accept your gift of abundant life however you give it to us. In your way, in your time, restore us to full health and wholeness. Amen.

**When they had prayed,
the place was shaken
where they were
assembled together; and
they were all filled with
the Holy Ghost, and
they spake the word of
God with boldness.**

—*ACTS 4:31*

I have resolved to pray more and pray always, to pray in all places where quietness inviteth: in the house, on the highway and on the street; and to know no street or passage in this city that may not witness that I have not forgotten God. I purpose to take occasion of praying upon the sight of any church which I may pass, that God may be worshipped there in spirit, and that souls my be saved there; to pray for my sick patients and for the patients of other physicians; at my entrance into any home to say, ...May the peace of God abide here.
—Sir Thomas Browne, 1605

He was wounded for our transgressions, he was bruised for our iniquities: the chastisement of our peace was upon him; and with his stripes we are healed.

—*ISAIAH 53:5*

IT takes great courage to heal, Lord, great energy to reach out from this darkness and ask for healing. Bless the brave voices telling nightmare tales of dreadful wounds to the gifted healers of this world. Together, sufferers and healers are binding up damaged parts and laying down burdens carried so long.

66

Heal the sick, cleanse the lepers, raise the dead, cast out devils: freely ye have received, freely give.

—*MATTHEW 10:8*

BLESS those who tend us when we are ailing in body, mind, and soul. They are a gift from you, Great Healer, sent to accompany us along the scary roads of illness. Bless their skills, potions, and bedside manners. Sustain them as they sustain us, for they are a channel of your love.

The prayer of faith shall save the sick, and the Lord shall raise him up; and if he have committed sins, they shall be forgiven him.

—*JAMES 5:15*

PRAYER is powerful. God hears prayer and heals his people. But this is more than healing our physical bodies. He is mostly concerned about our spiritual health. Confessing, forgiving sins, and praying for others has much to do with their spirit and soul—and ours. Clearly he wants to heal all of us—body, mind, and soul.

**Unless the Lord
had been my
help, my soul
had almost dwelt
in silence.**

—*PSALM 94:17*

THE silence of which the Psalmist speaks
is death. The land of silence is the grave.
We would probably all be dead if the Lord
had not helped us. Think of all the foolish
and even dangerous choices you've made.
Then thank a sovereign and merciful God
that he has preserved you and helped you.
Our very lived experience proves it is
true: our very life is a gift.

66

He shall judge among many people, and rebuke strong nations afar off; and they shall beat their swords into plowshares, and their spears into pruninghooks: nation shall not lift up a sword against nation, neither shall they learn war any more. But they shall sit every man under his vine and under his fig tree; and none shall make them afraid: for the mouth of the Lord of hosts hath spoken it.

—MICAH 4:3–4

GOD will judge the nations. We can be sure of that. But that's not the end of the story, is it? Peace and prosperity will follow, and that's the point. God's sovereign, righteous judgment ultimately ends our fear of danger or deprivation. None shall make us afraid. The Lord of hosts has said so. And that's enough.

Arise, O Lord; O God, lift up thine hand: forget not the humble.

—*PSALM 10:12*

SOMETIMES it seems to me that the selfish and wicked flourish, while everyone else struggles. We see people who have done great harm to others, who still retain their status and wealth and comfortable lifestyle. We call to God to make it right somehow. God, we know you judge all situations fairly and justly, seeing factors we're not aware of. Let us please trust in you, that you do remember the humble. Let us trust in your justice and your timing and your love.

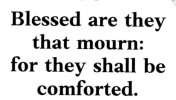

**Blessed are they
that mourn:
for they shall be
comforted.**

—*MATTHEW 5:4*

LORD, you know how all-encompassing grief can be. The weight we carry is physical as well as emotional, and even getting up in the morning can seem like an impossible, pointless act. Thank you, Lord, for bringing us comfort during such times. Eventually the day comes when we have the pleasant realization that we actually feel a little invigorated. We hold our heads a little higher as you help us find joy in our memories and peace in the knowledge that our loved one is safe by your side, looking down on us over your shoulder.

66

**Let us therefore
come boldly unto
the throne of
grace, that we may
obtain mercy, and
find grace to help
in time of need.**

—*HEBREWS 4:16*

NO one wants a health problem with an uncertain diagnosis. No one wants to wait and go through numerous tests to see if something is serious or not. Lord, please help me through this time of need. I pray that there will be nothing to this health scare—but if there is something wrong, please grant me the grace to accept the change and stress.

When thou prayest, enter into thy closet, and when thou hast shut thy door, pray to thy Father which is in secret; and thy Father which seeth in secret shall reward thee openly. But when ye pray, use not vain repetitions, as the heathen do: for they think that they shall be heard for their much speaking. Be not ye therefore like unto them: for your Father knoweth what things ye have need of, before ye ask him.

—*MATTHEW 6:6–8*

PRAYER does not have to be formal and structured in order to be effective. Just sit quietly, let your mind be still, share your thoughts with God, and listen to the wisdom in your heart.

"

If any of you lack wisdom, let him ask of God, that giveth to all men liberally, and upbraideth not; and it shall be given him. But let him ask in faith, nothing wavering. For he that wavereth is like a wave of the sea driven with the wind and tossed.
—*JAMES 1:5–6*

FAITH is a commodity that cannot be purchased, traded, or sold. It is a treasure that cannot be claimed and put on display in a museum. It is a richness no amount of money can compare to. When you have faith, you have a power that can change night into day, move mountains, calm stormy seas. When you have faith, you can fall over and over again, only to get up each time more determined that ever to succeed, and you will succeed. For faith is God in action, and faith is available to anyone, rich, poor, young or old, as long as you believe.

"

He that tilleth his land shall be satisfied with bread: but he that followeth vain persons is void of understanding.

—*PROVERBS 12:11*

I do sometimes prefer frivolity and flattery to growing in the light of some uncomfortable truth, Lord. You can see where I'm prone to skirting the issues I need to deal with, and you know when I'm indulging in foolishness when I could be having a meaningful interaction with someone who walks in the truth. I know it's okay to have fun, but it's good for me to look in the mirror regularly as well. Grant me the grace to soak in the wisdom that will change me for the better.

"

**Fear ye not therefore,
ye are of more value
than many sparrows.**

—MATTHEW 10:31

LORD, you know I'm a little worried about finances this month. Please help me trust in you, that we'll get through this rough patch. Ease my fears and let me be happy for those ways in which I have enough. And help me never forget to be generous to others.

Ye were not redeemed with corruptible things, as silver and gold, from your vain conversation received by tradition from your fathers; But with the precious blood of Christ, as of a lamb without blemish and without spot.

—*1 PETER 1:18–19*

LORD, you know how much time and effort I put into surrounding myself with my favorite things. Sometimes I wonder if it's always worth it. Please help me sort out what's truly valuable and what I can do without. One thing I know is worth pursuing is the wisdom found in your Word. As I read it and your Spirit helps me to comprehend it, I feel rich indeed.

Watch and pray, that ye enter not into temptation: the spirit indeed is willing, but the flesh is weak.

—*MATTHEW 26:41*

GIVE me strength today to stand against temptation. Empower me with the faith that I can say no to things that don't add to my peace or happiness without guilt or regret. Give me, God, the courage to turn away from things that might bring fleeting pleasure, but may not be your will for me. I ask today in prayer for the strength to do what is right, what is just, and what is fair, even if I am tempted to cheat, lie, or take more than my fair share. Amen.

Lord, who shall abide in thy tabernacle? who shall dwell in thy holy hill? He that walketh uprightly, and worketh righteousness, and speaketh the truth in his heart.

—*PSALM 15:1–2*

GOD, sometimes I lie even to myself. I tell myself, "Oh, that wasn't a big deal," or "I can afford to skip prayer time, since I did this other good thing today." I hold unexamined grudges instead of trying to forgive. Let me speak truth both in my heart and on my tongue; purify my thoughts and my words. When I go to worship, I want it to be with a clean, still spirit that is open to your love.

He arose, and rebuked the wind, and said unto the sea, Peace, be still. And the wind ceased, and there was a great calm. And he said unto them, Why are ye so fearful? how is it that ye have no faith?

—*MARK 4:39–40*

WHY tornadoes, Lord? Why typhoons or fires? Why floods or earthquakes? Why devastating accidents or acts of terror, Lord? It's so hard to understand. Perhaps there is no way to find any sense in overwhelming circumstances. Perhaps it's about trusting in you, God, no matter what comes and leaving it in your hands, where it belongs because, in fact, you do really love us and care about us and will make things work out for us.

> **Lead me in thy truth, and teach me: for thou art the God of my salvation; on thee do I wait all the day.**
>
> —*PSALM 25:5*

WE are blinded by our sorrow. Lift our eyes and bless us, O Father, with a defiant hope, steadfast trust, and fire in the belly to emerge from this darkness victorious and whole once again, standing in the light you've given us.

The Lord shall fight for you, and ye shall hold your peace.

—*EXODUS 14:14*

LORD, it's so easy to fight back. When threatened, I want to lash out, to get even, and to have the last word. Help me to hold my peace. If my cause is just, you will fight for me, as you did for the Hebrews fleeing the bondage of Egypt. While waiting for your deliverance, I can be silent. You are sovereign and I am safe, standing by the Red Sea waiting for a miracle.

66

**Put on therefore,
as the elect of
God, holy and
beloved, bowels of
mercies, kindness,
humbleness of
mind, meekness,
longsuffering.**

—*COLOSSIANS 3:12*

TODAY has not been a horrible day, but it has not been a good one either. I've been snappish and irritable, having to work hard to be kind to my coworkers, patient with my children, loving to my spouse. There's no particular reason why—just one of those days. Lord, please let me act with love—with patience, with kindness, with self-control—even when I'm feeling small and petty.

JULY 30

> **Peter said unto them, Repent, and be baptized every one of you in the name of Jesus Christ for the remission of sins, and ye shall receive the gift of the Holy Ghost.**
>
> —*ACTS 2:38*

WHEN we forgive, our hearts are lightened. It has taken me much of my adult life to understand that basic premise. And even now, I can approach forgiveness from the standpoint of the gift I'm giving another. It is only after I have forgiven someone, and my spirit lifts, that I remember, again: I benefit as much, if not more, than the person I've pardoned. Dear Lord, thank you for the gift you give freely each time I am moved to absolve another. Thank you for rewarding forgiveness by enriching my heart spiritually.

Lift up the hands which hang down, and the feeble knees; And make straight paths for your feet, lest that which is lame be turned out of the way; but let it rather be healed.

—*HEBREWS 12:12–13*

GOD's Spirit offers us the blessing of inner peace.

WALK WITH GOD

AUGUST

> **Nevertheless I am continually with thee: thou hast holden me by my right hand. Thou shalt guide me with thy counsel, and afterward receive me to glory.**
>
> —*PSALM 73:23–24*

LOOK around, for signs of God's presence are in the sky, the trees, the flowers in the fields, in the people you love, and the pets you hold dear. God's unceasing love is all around us if we stop long enough to behold his wonders!

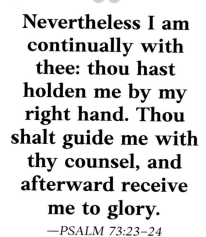

66

Teach us to number our days, that we may apply our hearts unto wisdom.

—*PSALM 90:12*

I watch the days of my life fly by, always thinking of what I need to do tomorrow, next week, next month. God, help me to slow down and take it all one step at a time, and drink in every present moment, for these moments will never come again.

> **Whereas ye know not what shall be on the morrow. For what is your life? It is even a vapour, that appeareth for a little time, and then vanisheth away.**
>
> —*JAMES 4:14*

GOD, please remind me throughout my day that the moment is all I have in which to live. I can't retrieve or retract anything I've done or said just ten minutes ago. Nor can I be sure of what will happen ten minutes hence. So I pray, Lord, help me leave the past and the future with you so that I can experience the peace of your love in this important bit of eternity called "now."

> **I must work the works of him that sent me, while it is day: the night cometh, when no man can work.**
>
> —*JOHN 9:4*

MY job is to do what God asks of me. That's it. I am not expected to go the full distance in one day. All God wants is for me to take that first step, and he will do the rest when he is ready.

66

And it came to pass, that, when Elisabeth heard the salutation of Mary, the babe leaped in her womb; and Elisabeth was filled with the Holy Ghost.

—*LUKE 1:41*

MARY and her cousin turned to each other for support during life-changing events. They sought to help and encourage each other. When I am feeling overwhelmed and unsure, let me reach out—to seek advice, but also to celebrate with others in their own milestones.

66

**The child grew,
and waxed strong
in spirit, filled
with wisdom: and
the grace of God
was upon him.**

—*LUKE 2:40*

JESUS, we think of you as an adult,
in your public ministry. But you went
through everything that we went
through, all the small joys and miseries
of childhood. I ask your blessing today on
those children I know, that they too will
grow strong in spirit and wisdom.

66

When I was a child, I spake as a child, I understood as a child, I thought as a child: but when I became a man, I put away childish things.

—*1 CORINTHIANS 13:11*

REFOCUS me, God of love, to embrace and enjoy this child growing so quickly into independence. When growth pains come, send me a rainbow of friends' support, vision, and patience to enjoy, although it's sure to rain again. Help me accept storm and sun as the balance of nature, of life.

66

Trust ye in the Lord for ever: for in the Lord Jehovah is everlasting strength.

—ISAIAH 26:4

I may not understand your ways, God, or what your plans are for me, but I trust you. I know you have my best interest always at heart, and you won't lead me astray. My trust in your will acts like a lighthouse beacon guiding me safely to shore.

"

Ye shall be clean: from all your filthiness, and from all your idols, will I cleanse you. A new heart also will I give you, and a new spirit will I put within you: and I will take away the stony heart out of your flesh, and I will give you an heart of flesh. And I will put my spirit within you, and cause you to walk in my statutes, and ye shall keep my judgments, and do them.

—*EZEKIEL 36:25–27*

HEAVENLY Father, your grace washes over me today, taking away all my impurities. I praise your name as I revel in your love. Please let me soak in the promise of eternal life in you, as I feel it penetrate my body to the very core. I want to carry that promise with me always, so as soon as I close my eyes, I can sense your Holy Spirit wrapped around me, holding me safe.

> **He giveth more grace.
> Wherefore he saith, God
> resisteth the proud, but
> giveth grace unto the humble.**
>
> —*JAMES 4:6*

I do things I am proud of now and then, but I have to remember that any pride I have belongs to God. It humbles me when I realize that by myself I can do nothing, but with God all things become possible. My successes are his successes. My accomplishments are his accomplishments. God, I pray you keep me humble enough to know who deserves the gratitude for all my blessings and miracles. Keep me wise enough to recognize your grace working in my life and not take credit for it myself. Pride limits me, but living in your will gives me unlimited access to the promises of the kingdom of heaven. May I remain always your humble servant, God.

66

**The meek shall
inherit the earth;
and shall delight
themselves in
the abundance
of peace.**

—*PSALM 37:11*

MUCH later Jesus quotes this promise in
the Beatitudes, a series of blessings in his
famous Sermon on the Mount. It seems
unlikely, doesn't it? Meekness denotes
humility, not necessarily weakness.
When a strong person is humble, that's a
beautiful thing. When a weak person is
humble, that's also a beautiful thing. Those
are the ones who make peace. Those are
the ones who are blessed.

66

The Spirit also helpeth our infirmities: for we know not what we should pray for as we ought: but the Spirit itself maketh intercession for us with groanings which cannot be uttered.

—*ROMANS 8:26*

WHENEVER I make plans for anything in my life, I check with God in prayer first. If it rings true in my heart, which is where God speaks to me, I go for it. The ideas may be mine, but the inspiration and motivation to make them a reality come from God.

> **Let the word of Christ dwell in you richly in all wisdom; teaching and admonishing one another in psalms and hymns and spiritual songs, singing with grace in your hearts to the Lord.**
>
> —*COLOSSIANS 3:16*

LORD, I ask for insight when I read the Bible. Let me not dismiss those passages I don't understand, or that I find difficult. Let your words transform me from within and build me up, drawing me more deeply into connection with you.

> **Brethren, I commend you to God, and to the word of his grace, which is able to build you up, and to give you an inheritance among all them which are sanctified.**
>
> —*ACTS 20:32*

THERE are times in our lives when we feel alone and abandoned. Our fate seems to be a foreboding place at the end of a long, dark road. But then something happens—a simple and small miracle occurs—that brings us back to the understanding that God is always in our lives and is always ready to be of help and support when we need it. Grace is God's gift to us; it is the blessing of his light being shined upon us as we stand in darkness. We know when God's grace has touched us because everything changes, and we change, and suddenly life seems a bit brighter and lighter than before.

66

**For thus saith the Lord
God, the Holy One of Israel;
In returning and rest shall
ye be saved; in quietness
and in confidence shall be
your strength.**

—*ISAIAH 30:15*

MAY you recognize today that not all
being-alone is loneliness, and not all
solitude is a problem to solve. With
everyone far away, rejoice in the blessing
of quietness.

> **He healeth the broken in heart, and bindeth up their wounds.**
>
> —*PSALM 147:3*

COMFORT, dear God, those whose eyes are filled with tears and those whose backs are near breaking with the weight of a heavy burden. Heal those whose hearts hold a wound and whose faith has been dealt a blow. Bless all who mourn and who despair. Help those who can't imagine how they'll make it through another day. For your goodness and mercy are enough for all the troubles in the world. Amen.

66

The sufferings of this present time are not worthy to be compared with the glory which shall be revealed in us.

—*ROMANS 8:18*

LORD, I know that part of life is loss and that without loss we cannot treasure the new blessings that come our way. But I am still hurting, and the pain is deep. Help me see the beautiful silver lining that surrounds the dark clouds now hanging overhead. Amen.

> **I know thy works, and tribulation, and poverty, (but thou art rich).**
>
> —*REVELATION 2:9*

JUST because God's way of helping us is different than we hoped or expected, it doesn't mean he is indifferent to our cries for help. We must believe that he knows what is truly best for us and is actively doing what is best for us.

> **But the wisdom that is from above is first pure, then peaceable, gentle, and easy to be intreated, full of mercy and good fruits, without partiality, and without hypocrisy.**
>
> —*JAMES 3:17*

I seek the wisdom of understanding, and the grace of peace. The world is becoming a hostile place and only those armed with your loving care seem able to find their way, and then light the way for others who are lost in the darkness. I ask from you a strong center from which I may go forth into the world and spread that same peace and that same understanding to others that need it so badly. Make me an instrument of your peace today, dear Lord. Let me help others find their center within where you reside, always loving, always caring, and forever present. Amen.

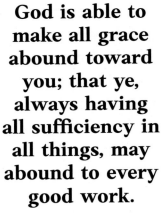

**God is able to
make all grace
abound toward
you; that ye,
always having
all sufficiency in
all things, may
abound to every
good work.**

—*2 CORINTHIANS 9:8*

GREAT are the blessings of those who
have peace in Christ.

> **The seed shall be prosperous; the vine shall give her fruit, and the ground shall give her increase, and the heavens shall give their dew; and I will cause the remnant of this people to possess all these things.**
>
> —*ZECHARIAH 8:12*

THIS is my benediction upon you: that peace be with you all the days of your life, and that you dwell in the house of the Lord forever.

> **Be glad in the Lord, and rejoice, ye righteous: and shout for joy, all ye that are upright in heart.**
>
> —*PSALM 32:11*

FATHER, instill in me the gifts of humor and joy. Teach me how to lift downcast spirits and dispense the medicine of good cheer in your name.

66

**Above all things
have fervent charity
among yourselves:
for charity shall
cover the multitude
of sins.**

—*1 PETER 4:8*

BE ready to offer your gentle touch
today—and celebrate the gift of kindness.
Reach out to the elderly and infirm.
Stretch out your hand to the children and
infants. Do not hold back. Celebrate by
letting your warmth flow through. And
rejoice in your ability to do God's will in
this way.

> **Bless the Lord, O my soul, and forget not all his benefits: Who forgiveth all thine iniquities; who healeth all thy diseases; Who redeemeth thy life from destruction; who crowneth thee with lovingkindness and tender mercies.**
>
> —*PSALM 103:2–4*

LORD, make me aware of your benefits. This verse lists only a few, but I thank you today for forgiveness, health, redemption, and mercy. Your lovingkindness overwhelms me—if only I pause and contemplate how vast and rich it is. And how complete. You forgive all my iniquities and heal all my diseases, in your own time and in your own way. For this my very soul blesses you. Help me be more like you, extending love and mercy to my coworkers, friends, and family.

> 66

I have filled him with the spirit of God, in wisdom, and in understanding, and in knowledge, and in all manner of workmanship, To devise cunning works, to work in gold, and in silver, and in brass, And in cutting of stones, to set them, and in carving of timber, to work in all manner of workmanship.

—*EXODUS 31:3–5*

YOU can have those dreams you dream. God instilled them in you so you could express his love out into the world. Through your skills, talent, and creativity, God wants you to be epic! Make plans, and then let him work those plans through you in a miraculous way!

> **Seest thou a man diligent in his business? he shall stand before kings; he shall not stand before mean men.**
>
> —*PROVERBS 22:29*

TO have talent and not use it is to ignore the calling of a higher voice. To be given gifts and not share them is to nullify the moving of spirit through the soul as it seeks to be made manifest in the outer world. We are given our light to let it shine, not to hide it from others for fear of drawing attention. For when we shine, we allow others to do so as well. God did not make stars in order to keep them from glowing in the night sky, nor did he make birds in order to keep them grounded. When we open our storehouse of talents and treasures, the whole world benefits and is made brighter.

> ❝

**The Lord will
give strength
unto his people;
the Lord will
bless his people
with peace.**

—*PSALM 29:11*

GOD strengthens individuals, but he also strengthens groups. This thought gave me comfort last night as I prepared for a summer mission trip. I will be traveling to Oklahoma to help rebuild homes destroyed in a tornado, and have been charged with directing eight college-aged kids from my church. I am a skilled carpenter but less certain about leading a group. God, I pray you will grant my team the strength and cohesiveness we need to do our jobs well.

> **Art thou the Christ? tell us. And he said unto them, If I tell you, ye will not believe: And if I also ask you, ye will not answer me, nor let me go. Hereafter shall the Son of man sit on the right hand of the power of God.**
>
> —*LUKE 22:67–69*

HOW joyful life becomes when we surrender to our faith in God, allowing his will to work through us. We give up resistance and frustration, and things suddenly seem to flow with greater ease. We still have obstacles, but also the strength and resources to overcome them. Living in faith and experiencing more peace and joy is what God intended for us!

> **Take heed to yourselves: for they shall deliver you up to councils; and in the synagogues ye shall be beaten: and ye shall be brought before rulers and kings for my sake, for a testimony against them. And the gospel must first be published among all nations.**
>
> —MARK 13:9–10

IT is easy to have faith when things are going well, when the bills are paid and everyone is happy and in good health. But blessed is the person who has steadfast and unmoving faith when everything is going wrong. That's when faith is most needed—and least employed. If a person can suspend all intellectual judgment and look beyond the illusion of negative appearances, faith will begin to move mountains. By putting the mighty power to work, faith will begin to work some mighty powerful miracles in your life.

> **For we walk by faith, not by sight.**
> —*2 CORINTHIANS 5:7*

MY daughter loves the stories about Jesus and the miracles he wrought: water into wine, healing the sick. "Why don't we see miracles like this anymore?" she asked me just yesterday. I too have yearned to see visible signs of God's presence. But as my daughter and I talked, we began to acknowledge the presence of miracles in the everyday: the antibiotic she took last week for an ear infection; the rosemary seeds we'd planted together, which are gaining traction and sprouting up. Health and new life burgeon behind the scenes: our world is, in fact, full of miracles! And when we cannot recognize them for the miracles they are? Then we must rely on faith. God, help me to see the miracles in my life, and strengthen me to have faith even when I don't see visible signs of your presence.

Thou wilt keep him in perfect peace, whose mind is stayed on thee: because he trusteth in thee.

—ISAIAH 26:3

WHAT a wonderful day! And now, God of rest and peace, the children are sleeping, replete with the joys of our summer discoveries that they are savoring to the last drop. We celebrate the joy of ordinary days and rest in your care.

WALK WITH GOD

SEPTEMBER

66

**Through the tender
mercy of our God;
whereby the dayspring
from on high hath
visited us, To give
light to them that sit
in darkness and in the
shadow of death, to
guide our feet into the
way of peace.**

—LUKE 1:78–79

THOSE who love the paths of peace will
walk in them.

66

Go ye therefore, and teach all nations, baptizing them in the name of the Father, and of the Son, and of the Holy Ghost: Teaching them to observe all things whatsoever I have commanded you: and, lo, I am with you always, even unto the end of the world. Amen.

—*MATTHEW 28:19–20*

WHEN I follow God's will and do as he instructs me, my direction becomes clear as I step out onto the path. I look around and see his presence everywhere, guiding me forward to where my spirit longs to be. I see his signs showing me the way.

> **I am the vine, ye are the branches: He that abideth in me, and I in him, the same bringeth forth much fruit: for without me ye can do nothing.**
>
> *—JOHN 15:5*

AS Jesus continues to comfort his disciples, he promises they will bear much fruit—if they abide in him. Abiding is the thing, then. The image he uses is that of a vine. Sustenance flows through him to us—and then the branches flourish. We know they flourish because there is "much fruit." He explains how this works in verse 7: "If ye abide in me, and my words abide in you, ye shall ask what ye will, and it shall be done unto you." Knowing his Word changes what we want, and it changes what we get. What we get is "the peaceable fruit of righteousness" (Hebrews 12:11). It becomes what we want too.

66

Counsel is mine, and sound wisdom: I am understanding; I have strength.

—*PROVERBS 8:14*

LET me do what lies clearly at hand, this very minute. Grant me the insight to see that too much planning for the future removes me from the present moment. And this is the only existence, the only calling I have been given—right now— to do what is necessary. Nothing more, nothing less. Thus may I use this next moment wisely.

"

If it be possible, as much as lieth in you, live peaceably with all men. Dearly beloved, avenge not yourselves, but rather give place unto wrath: for it is written, Vengeance is mine; I will repay, saith the Lord. Therefore if thine enemy hunger, feed him; if he thirst, give him drink: for in so doing thou shalt heap coals of fire on his head.

—*ROMANS 12:18–20*

HEADLINES depress us with money problems, strife, and school problems; with housing, family, and health problems. We need sunshine to bring everything to light. Send the sun's light through creation: surf and skyline merging, bird song and flight. Send it through people: friends who laugh at our jokes, family who never stray. Send it through inner knowing: unexplained peace and joy, faith that you're working alongside us. Lord, we celebrate your truth.

66

**Have mercy upon
me, O Lord; for I
am weak: O Lord,
heal me; for my
bones are vexed.**

—*PSALM 6:2*

TAKING care of ourselves is the first step.
Letting others care for us is the next step.
But much of the journey toward healing
happens when we allow God to step into
our lives.

66

When he was now not far from the house, the centurion sent friends to him, saying unto him, Lord, trouble not thyself: for I am not worthy that thou shouldest enter under my roof: Wherefore neither thought I myself worthy to come unto thee: but say in a word, and my servant shall be healed.

—*LUKE 7:6–7*

LORD, the trust of the centurion was incredible. Like him, let me trust that you are working in my life, not asking for signs or worrying about the progress of some problem, but trusting that the matter is safe in your hands, and you will heal whatever needs to be healed.

66

When thou liest down, thou shalt not be afraid: yea, thou shalt lie down, and thy sleep shall be sweet.

—PROVERBS 3:24

DEAR God,

The long and loud and noisy day threatens to overwhelm me, and there are still so many hours to go before I sleep. Will it ever end? Will I ever know the precious sound of golden silence? God, give me the gift of inner peace so that no matter how loud the baby cries or how many times the phone rings or how grating the sound of my boss's voice gets in my ear, I will be able to crawl safe and secure into my inner sanctuary and find the renewal I need to do it all again tomorrow. Amen!

No man can serve two masters: for either he will hate the one, and love the other; or else he will hold to the one, and despise the other. Ye cannot serve God and mammon.

—*MATTHEW 6:24*

O Lord, how many distractions there are in this world! How easy it is for us to get caught up in the desire to acquire, moving from one purchase to the next. How tempting it is to read one self-help book after another, until we are dizzy. Lord, I know that true contentment, true beauty, and true wisdom are all found only in your Word. Protect me from focusing too much on material things.

66

All things were made by him; and without him was not any thing made that was made.

—*JOHN 1:3*

HOW different our lives would be without inventions! When I think back to what life must have been like one hundred years ago, I am grateful for the things that make my life easier. I am glad to have machines to help me cook, clean, and stay entertained. Thank you, God, for inspiring those who came up the inventions that make my life so much easier than my ancestors' lives.

66

**For the Lord
giveth wisdom:
out of his
mouth cometh
knowledge and
understanding.**
—*PROVERBS 2:6*

INTELLIGENCE is knowing with the mind. Wisdom is knowing with the heart. There are times in life when we must turn to the wisdom of our hearts for answers and direction, because the mind does not have that deeper knowing and understanding. Our hearts are the direct pipeline to God's loving wisdom, and only through the heart can we access it and put it to use in our lives.

66

Is this grace given [...] that now unto the principalities and powers in heavenly places might be known by the church the manifold wisdom of God.

—*EPHESIANS 3:8, 10*

GOD reveals his wisdom through his church. Somewhere in your neighborhood there is a group of imperfect people meeting together, seeking to know God and understand his Word. And he promises to use them to encourage each other in this desire.

> **Now therefore ye are no more strangers and foreigners, but fellow citizens with the saints, and of the household of God.**
>
> —*EPHESIANS 2:19*

COMMUNITY enriches us, granting us a sense of belonging, mutual support, and opportunities to exchange ideas and knowledge. But in today's transient culture, people move all the time. A move to a new place can be an exciting opportunity, of course. But uprooting from a familiar place, with its reassuring ties, can be unsettling. You had found someone who cut your hair just right; you knew who to call for home repair, or when the pipe under the sink sprouted a leak. Perhaps most importantly, you had a network of friends and loved ones who helped you feel at home in the world. It takes time to re-establish a sense of community after a move, but God is present to help us on the journey. In an unfamiliar place, have faith that you will find your people.

66

**We have as an anchor
of the soul, both sure
and stedfast, and which
entereth into that
within the veil.**

—HEBREWS 6:19

MAY your nerves hold out in this
transition! It's hectic making big changes.
It takes away the security, the comfort,
the sense of stability. We were made for
change, but we prefer the status quo. We
even begin to assume that where we make
our home can be heaven itself. But there is
only one true heaven.

> **" Now unto him that is able to do exceeding abundantly above all that we ask or think, according to the power that worketh in us, Unto him be glory in the church by Christ Jesus throughout all ages, world without end. Amen.**

—*EPHESIANS 3:20–21*

GOD is bigger than any problem you have. Whoever is opposing you is a weakling compared to God. Why not tap into God's supply of strength? Why focus on your problem when God is so much more interesting?

66

Or despisest thou the riches of his goodness and forbearance and longsuffering; not knowing that the goodness of God leadeth thee to repentance?

—*ROMANS 2:4*

NO matter how badly someone has sinned, the promise of God's love is enough to make them repent. I've seen this happen many times with people I never thought would change. But one experience of God's presence, and they did change, becoming renewed and reborn in spirit. God can do that. God can take what is dark in us and turn it to light. I pray, dear God, that you help those who most need it, and find those who are lost and alone. Lead them to the promise of your grace and mercy, and heal what is broken in them. The world is often a scary place. I pray, God, that you work your miracles in many hearts today.

66

A new commandment I give unto you, That ye love one another; as I have loved you, that ye also love one another.

—JOHN 13:34

COMFORT me in my day of need with a love that is infinite and true. Ignore my lack of desire to forgive and forget. Fill my anger with the waters of peace and serenity that I may come to accept this situation and move on to a greater level of understanding and knowing.

Behold, I will bring it health and cure, and I will cure them, and will reveal unto them the abundance of peace and truth.

—*JEREMIAH 33:6*

FATHER, thank you for helping me recognize my sadness. As I come to you for healing, I will keep sight of both the beginning and end of my sorrow. Amen.

66

**He said unto the man,
Stretch forth thy hand.
And he did so: and
his hand was restored
whole as the other.**

—*LUKE 6:10*

LORD, I ask for your restoration today.
Heal my body, my mind, and my soul from
injuries and old wounds. I hold out my
hands to you today.

66

**Immediately Jesus
stretched forth his hand,
and caught him, and
said unto him, O thou
of little faith, wherefore
didst thou doubt?**

—*MATTHEW 14:31*

SOMETIMES my doubts are so strong
and so bothersome. Give me courage
to express my doubts to you, O God,
knowing that they are necessary moments
through which I can pass on my way to
true contentment in you.

For the scripture saith, Whosoever believeth on him shall not be ashamed.

—*ROMANS 10:11*

LEAN on your faith when there is no one around to help. Like a strong pillar, faith in God can hold you up during the worst of storms and the harshest of winds. Faith gives you something to hold onto. Faith even brings you back home to God again when you are sure you are lost and alone.

To every thing there is a season, and a time to every purpose under the heaven.

—*ECCLESIASTES 3:1*

AS the seasons change and the exterior world becomes a different place, we can find the courage and power and guidance we need by staying focused on the unchangeable, unmovable, infinite center within.

"

The eyes of the Lord are in every place, beholding the evil and the good.

—*PROVERBS 15:3*

WHAT we cannot do for ourselves, God can do for us. With our limited vision and perception, only God's wisdom can look beyond our lack and limitations. How comforting is it to know that we have this resource to turn to anytime we need? God is always ready to help us, to advise us, and to direct us.

> **"**
>
> **The Lord is merciful and gracious, slow to anger, and plenteous in mercy. He will not always chide: neither will he keep his anger for ever. He hath not dealt with us after our sins; nor rewarded us according to our iniquities. For as the heaven is high above the earth, so great is his mercy toward them that fear him.**
>
> —PSALM 103:8–11

LORD, you have not dealt with me according to my sin, so great is your mercy toward them that fear you. Help me to treat others as you do, and to be as merciful and gracious to them as you are to me. Help me be slow to anger, and reluctant to chide. Help me be more like you today, not rewarding those around me according to their actions but by the standard of your mercy. Give me a clearer vision of yourself and help me reflect your mercy to those around me.

**Blessed are the
peacemakers:
for they shall
be called the
children of God.**

—*MATTHEW 5:9*

WHAT does it mean to be a peacemaker?
Not to overlook wrongs, or to speak
soothing platitudes, but to work out
conflicts by listening to God's will.
Bless those who do the difficult work of
restoring relationships in accordance with
God's plan.

66

For the kingdom of God is not meat and drink; but righteousness, and peace, and joy in the Holy Ghost.

—ROMANS 14:17

I work overtime to provide the best home I can for my family. I want the best for my children and that often means material things like clothing and school supplies. I am doing my best to teach them how to earn and save money on their own, but more importantly, I am teaching them to first work towards being happy and kind and to live in the spirit of God's will. I want to be an example for them of a person who knows the promises of God are more than just physical and material, but also of the spirit and soul. I pray, dear God, to be a guiding light for those aspiring to experience your unseen blessings and miracles.

66

Finally, my brethren, be strong in the Lord, and in the power of his might.

—EPHESIANS 6:10

I will not turn back. I will not give up. I will never surrender. With God at my side, I will simply step over obstacles, go around challenges, and break through blocks put in my path. With God, I am unstoppable!

"

**The people asked him,
saying, What shall we
do then? He answereth
and saith unto them,
He that hath two coats,
let him impart to him
that hath none; and he
that hath meat, let him
do likewise.**

—*LUKE 3:10–11*

DEAR heavenly Father, I truly want to do
good toward others. I don't want to just
talk about being good, but I desire to be
more compassionate. God, I need for you
to teach me to be far more sensitive to
the needs and sorrows of the people you
have placed in my life and to be kind and
encouraging toward them. I need for you
to teach me how to truly love. I pray for
this with all my heart. Amen.

Flee also youthful lusts: but follow righteousness, faith, charity, peace, with them that call on the Lord out of a pure heart.

—*2 TIMOTHY 2:22*

DEAR Lord,
I've been alone for a while now, and I would love someone special in my life to share my ups and downs and the experiences of being alive with. On my own, I am liable to pick someone who may not be the best for me, so I ask in prayer that you send to me the perfect mate, who is a lover, a friend, a partner and a confidante. I ask for someone I can trust and lean on and laugh with, and someone who shares my views and values, yet challenges me to always think beyond my own limited vision and be more of myself. Lord, direct my steps to this perfect love, one that is perfect for me in your view. I am ready to love, and to be loved. Amen.

> **He shall call upon
> me, and I will
> answer him:
> I will be with
> him in trouble;
> I will deliver him,
> and honour him.**
>
> —PSALM 91:15

THE Bible promises that God will always
be with us. Whether we are commuting
to work, having coffee with friends, taking
a walk, or even sleeping soundly through
the night—whatever it is, wherever we
are, he's there with us. He's the friend
who always has time, never moves to
another part of the world, is forever ready
to listen, and provides the best counsel.
It's just a matter of realizing he's there.

WALK WITH GOD

OCTOBER

"

Rejoice evermore. Pray without ceasing. In every thing give thanks: for this is the will of God in Christ Jesus concerning you.

—*1 THESSALONIANS 5:16–18*

BLESS me with silent conversations, O God, so I may be with you while doing chores, while singing in the shower, while brushing the cat. Sometimes words don't have to be spoken to be understood, and I get your message, too, in the silence that fills and comforts.

❝

He is the head of the body, the church: who is the beginning, the firstborn from the dead; that in all things he might have the preeminence.

—*COLOSSIANS 1:18*

BLESS us, Lord, as we go to worship this morning. Look down upon our efforts to honor your name through song and word and fellowship. And help us do it. For only in your power do we live and feel and move. And in your being alone do we find our true identity.

Wherefore we receiving a kingdom which cannot be moved, let us have grace, whereby we may serve God acceptably with reverence and godly fear.
—*HEBREWS 12:28*

I attend church regularly, but I find that the place I feel closest to God is in nature. As I walk through these trees, which existed before I was born and will stand tall long after my death, I am reminded of God's permanence. Being in the woods lifts my heart as I am surrounded by leafy evidence that God's presence is everlasting. During my walks, I talk to God about how grateful I am for the life he has given me and that I am still healthy enough to hike. I am also grateful that when my time on Earth is finally done, I will move on to a place where I will abide permanently in God's grace and love. Lord, thank you for recognizing the gratitude that underlies my worship in the woods.

He said unto them, Why are ye troubled? and why do thoughts arise in your hearts?

—*LUKE 24:38*

THANK you, my Lord, for helping me trust you enough to tear down walls of fear and doubt. Thank you for opening wide the door of my wounded heart so that I may love and praise you.

**For God hath
not given us the
spirit of fear; but
of power, and
of love, and of a
sound mind.**

—*2 TIMOTHY 1:7*

YOU may be afraid, but you've got the power of God on your side. So stand up and be the fullest and deepest expression of yourself you can possibly be. Let God do his will in your life and light up the world with your brilliance, your talents, and the gifts only you can give!

**See that none
render evil for
evil unto any man;
but ever follow
that which is
good, both among
yourselves, and to
all men.**

—*1 THESSALONIANS 5:15*

LORD, you who brought peace in the midst of the storm are the only one who can bring peace to our world today. How much anger we see raging around us, Lord. And the conflicts are not limited to wars on foreign soil. Rather they rage in the hearts and minds of many of us. Be the source of peace in every gathering storm, Lord. You are the Prince of Peace, and we need you desperately.

66

Love your enemies, do good to them which hate you, Bless them that curse you, and pray for them which despitefully use you. And unto him that smiteth thee on the one cheek offer also the other; and him that taketh away thy cloak forbid not to take thy coat also.

—*LUKE 6:27–29*

LORD, you know I have been dealing with someone with a difficult personality. Whatever our issues, help me be charitable in my thoughts and words. Please extend your grace over both of us, and send your Holy Spirit to inspire us both to kindness. Please help me remember that you want this person to be loving and whole in you, not isolated and alone. Please grant us a way to walk in harmony with you and each other.

**Thou shalt not
avenge, nor bear
any grudge against
the children of
thy people, but
thou shalt love thy
neighbour as thyself:
I am the Lord.**

—*LEVITICUS 19:18*

LORD, help us move beyond the times we hurt one another, the times we willingly misunderstand, the times we cherish our differences, and the times we assume we know all there is to know about each other and turn away. Amen.

A soft answer turneth away wrath: but grievous words stir up anger.

—PROVERBS 15:1

LET me know the satisfaction of forgiving today, O Lord. I have held my peace, doused my anger. Now it is time to extend my hand.

These things I have spoken unto you, that in me ye might have peace. In the world ye shall have tribulation: but be of good cheer; I have overcome the world.

—*JOHN 16:33*

LORD, we stand on your promises, but when it comes to your promise that your peace is with us, we sometimes stand confused. Where is your peace when young soldiers are killed in war? Where is your peace in the middle of the night when a sick child cannot be comforted? Where is your peace when a marriage is irretrievably broken? Yet even when we cannot see your peace, Lord, we know it is there because of your promise. We can find it in these and all circumstances when we come to you humbly and ask you for it. Thank you for your unfailing promise of peace. Amen.

> **Ye shall receive power, after that the Holy Ghost is come upon you: and ye shall be witnesses unto me both in Jerusalem, and in all Judaea, and in Samaria, and unto the uttermost part of the earth.**
>
> —*ACTS 1:8*

DEAR God, when obstacles threaten to derail me from the path towards my goals, give me the strength to go forward anyway, even if it means taking a little detour. Help me keep my pace, and not become weak of body or spirit over the long road ahead.

Ye shall serve the Lord your God, and he shall bless thy bread, and thy water; and I will take sickness away from the midst of thee.

—*EXODUS 23:25*

CHRONIC pain is not easy to deal with. You know, Father God, that I constantly fight discouragement, that I feel trapped by this contrary body. Please grant me a little grace today, to set my focus on others, and on you.

**For which cause
we faint not; but
though our outward
man perish, yet
the inward man is
renewed day by day.**

—*2 CORINTHIANS 4:16*

I'VE set a single place at the table, O God, and am dining alone this first time without my companion, my friend. What can we say to bless this lonely meal? What words can we use to grace this half-portion of life? Be with me as I swallow around lonely tears. Bless my remembering; inspire me to care for myself in honor of all the love that went before. From now on, I will set places in my heart for Memory and Hope, new companions for my table.

**I thank my God upon
every remembrance
of you, Always in
every prayer of mine
for you all making
request with joy.**

—*PHILIPPIANS 1:3–4*

HOW blessed are the good memories,
Lord! In fact, I am beginning to see that
my happiness can consist largely in the
looking back. For that I am grateful, as
I lay here, unable for the moment to be
active. Thank you for filling my heart.

I know that there is no good in them, but for a man to rejoice, and to do good in his life.

—*ECCLESIASTES 3:12*

MAY you learn to let your happiness depend, day by day, not upon something you could possibly lose, but upon that which could never, ever pass away.

**The earth and all
the inhabitants
thereof are
dissolved: I bear
up the pillars of it.**

—*PSALM 75:3*

IN the end, our God is the pillar that
upholds all we know and love and do.
He is the foundation of it, the support
that holds everything together. When
things seem to be falling apart, when our
worlds dissolve, he will bear us up. When
others fail us and circumstances disappoint
us, he is steadfast and strong. The only
strength we need is his strength and he
will not crumble.

The Lord is my helper, and I will not fear what man shall do unto me.

—HEBREWS 13:6

OUR worries are hard to dismiss, Lord. They seem to grow bigger and bigger until they take over our lives. Please help us conquer them, one at a time. Your reassurance is welcome. Amen.

Search me, O God, and know my heart: try me, and know my thoughts.

—*PSALM 139:23*

FROM the moment I got up to make coffee, I was filled with a pervasive sense of anxiety. I tried to take care, giving myself extra time for my commute to work, and organizing my day to minimize stress. And yet nothing seemed to help until I had the sense to close my office door, put my phone aside, and say the quiet, simple prayer, "Help." I won't tell you that my anxiety magically went away, for it did not. But I had a moment to collect myself, to register some of the things that had piled up throughout the week—a bad grade my son earned in math, the leaky faucet, the fact that I haven't been sleeping as well—and the understanding gave me some context, and consequently some relief. God, thank you for being there to guide me.

The God of peace shall bruise Satan under your feet shortly.

—ROMANS 16:20

GOD had to crush Satan before we could have peace. We understand that—it is the message of the cross. But in this context, it signifies the divisions between God's people that must be resolved. Satan is stirring up controversy in the church at Rome. False teachers "by good words and fair speeches deceive the hearts of the simple" (verse 18). What the Apostle Paul is promising his readers is that God will take care of this. God's peace and power will prevail—that's just what happens. So "mark them which cause divisions and offences contrary to the doctrine which ye have learned; and avoid them," he urges (verse 17). But you don't need to argue with them. It's under control.

Wherefore, my beloved brethren, let every man be swift to hear, slow to speak, slow to wrath: For the wrath of man worketh not the righteousness of God.

—*JAMES 1:19–20*

MY anger is all consuming and my fantasies are flamed by satisfying thoughts of revenge. Then, like a rustle of wind across a wheat field, I hear you reminding me that healing from violence is an issue of ecology. Is seeking revenge putting my time and energy to good use? Dear Lord, I am down on my knees with this one: Shall I rebuild or retaliate?

If thou, Lord, shouldest mark iniquities, O Lord, who shall stand? But there is forgiveness with thee, that thou mayest be feared.

—*PSALM 130:3–4*

FEW promises bring as much comfort as this one: there is forgiveness in the Lord. We cannot stand in God's presence, so great is our failure and sin. Like Isaiah we fall on our faces before the holiness of God. We say, "Woe is me! [...] for mine eyes have seen the King, the Lord of hosts" (Isaiah 6:5). And yet there is forgiveness. The seraphim flies from the altar before the throne of God and says, "Thine iniquity is taken away, and thy sin purged" (Isaiah 6:7). What freedom there is in this! And what fear as well. We are awed because "with the Lord there is mercy, and with him is plenteous redemption" (Psalm 130:7). Who could stand if the Lord should mark our iniquities without extending his forgiveness?

Blessed are the merciful: for they shall obtain mercy.

—MATTHEW 5:7

LORD, your forgiveness, based on your love for me, has transformed my life. I've experienced inner healing and freedom in knowing that you have wiped my slate clean and made me your friend. Help me to become an extension of your love to those around me. Let healing happen as I apply the salve to the wounds they inflict on me. Please strengthen me while I carry it out in your name. Amen.

**Who his own self
bare our sins in his
own body on the tree,
that we, being dead
to sins, should live
unto righteousness:
by whose stripes ye
were healed.**

—*1 PETER 2:24*

WHEN each heartbeat hurts and each
breath aches, I pray, God, that you will
take some of my blinding pain away. Lift
me out of my pain, comfort me, and give
me peace. Amen.

Defend the poor and fatherless: do justice to the afflicted and needy.

—*PSALM 82:3*

DEAR heavenly Father, today, if I see or hear of someone who is struggling in some way, please help me take a moment to remember what it was like when I was struggling and you helped me through the aid of a friend or stranger. Let that memory mobilize me to offer help and be your true servant. This I pray. Amen.

For whatsoever things were written aforetime were written for our learning, that we through patience and comfort of the scriptures might have hope.

—ROMANS 15:4

WE all have days when nothing goes right, and all we want to do is crawl back to bed and curl up into a ball. Sometimes those days stretch into weeks and months of bleak depression. But God is always there, watching over us, gently urging us to have hope because he has a plan for us. We may not see it unfolding, but it is, and hope is the pathway there.

Jesus said unto him, If thou canst believe, all things are possible to him that believeth.

—*MARK 9:23*

WHAT does it mean to have faith? It means moving through the challenges of daily life with boldness because we know that someone has our back. It means approaching life's obstacles with courage and conviction because we know someone is looking out for us. It means walking with our heads held high because we know someone walks alongside us. That someone is God.

God is in the midst of her; she shall not be moved: God shall help her, and that right early.

—*PSALM 46:5*

DEAR Lord, my daughter's school life has been miserable lately. For the past four years, she and two other girls have been inseparable. Birthday parties, sleepovers, movie dates: When two of them gather, it's been a given that the third will be invited to join. But this year, something changed: A new girl joined the group, and my daughter has started to feel marginalized. Last week, the other three went shopping and "forgot" to invite her. When she went to a sleepover, the other girls had a series of private jokes to which my daughter wasn't privy. My heart bleeds for her, and sometimes I have a hard time masking my own anger at the situation. God, please help me to remain strong so that I can help my daughter navigate these difficulties with grace.

**Behold, what
manner of love
the Father hath
bestowed upon us,
that we should be
called the sons of
God: therefore the
world knoweth
us not, because it
knew him not.**

—*1 JOHN 3:1*

MAY you come to know that God is your friend. When you feel a frowning face is looking down at you from heaven, recall that nothing you could do could ever make God love you more or love you less. He simply loves—completely, perfectly. So feel the blessedness of that!

But thou, O Lord, art a shield for me; my glory, and the lifter up of mine head.

—PSALM 3:3

IT seems like every week brings a barrage of bad news for myself, my family, my friends, and my community. When I am feeling overwhelmed, let me remember that you are with me at all times. You are my shield, Lord. Protected by you, I can face anything.

Without faith it is impossible to please him: for he that cometh to God must believe that he is, and that he is a rewarder of them that diligently seek him.

—*HEBREWS 11:6*

GOD, I ask for a bold and courageous faith to get me through these trials and tribulations. Let me stand on my own feet, but steady my footing with the knowledge of your presence. Give me the strength of will to never give up, no matter how crazy life gets.

> **Say to them that are
> of a fearful heart,
> Be strong, fear not:
> behold, your God will
> come with vengeance,
> even God with a
> recompence; he will
> come and save you.**

—*ISAIAH 35:4*

LORD, fear has reared its ugly head again and is trying to take me far away from you. Hold me close, Lord. Even though I have momentarily lost my footing in this world, please do not let fear steal the peace I find in you. Give me the strength to turn away from fear and stand tall in the knowledge that I am never alone.

WALK WITH GOD

NOVEMBER

With the ancient is wisdom; and in length of days understanding.

—*JOB 12:12*

I can only achieve so much without looking to those who have come before me. God has given me the gift of wisdom by placing people in my life who have the experience and insights I seek.

> **"**
>
> **The Lord is my strength and song, and he is become my salvation: he is my God, and I will prepare him an habitation; my father's God, and I will exalt him.**
>
> —*EXODUS 15:2*

YOUR changes touch my life with hope and mystery. God of love and power, I come today ready and eager to experience your power working through me.

**Above all, taking
the shield of faith,
wherewith ye shall
be able to quench
all the fiery darts of
the wicked.**

—EPHESIANS 6:16

WHEN I can see no way out of the dark
tunnel of despair, my faith becomes the
bright beacon of light that guides my path.
When I can feel no end to the pain I am
suffering, my faith becomes the soothing
balm that brings relief. My faith in God
never disappoints me or abandons me.
Even though I cannot see it, I know it is
always at work in my life.

> He staggered not at the promise of God through unbelief; but was strong in faith, giving glory to God; And being fully persuaded that, what he had promised, he was able also to perform.

—*ROMANS 4:20–21*

THERE is a difference between wishing that something was so and having faith that it will be. Wishing implies an attitude of hope based on fantasy and daydreams. Faith implies an attitude of belief based upon reality and intentions. You can wish for a thing all you want, but until you have complete faith that it can—and will—be yours, it will be just a wish.

66

Hearken therefore unto the supplications of thy servant, and of thy people Israel, which they shall make toward this place: hear thou from thy dwelling place, even from heaven; and when thou hearest, forgive.

—2 CHRONICLES 6:21

I need to talk to you, Lord, but when and where? When life offers few prayable moments, lead me to a quiet spirit spot at work or home—or caught in traffic between the two. Briefly is enough time until we have more.

For his anger endureth but a moment; in his favour is life: weeping may endure for a night, but joy cometh in the morning.

—*PSALM 30:5*

MY Creator, I know in my heart that these tears will one day give way again to joy, yet for now I know only pain. Help me to find the courage to let these tears flow, to feel the loss and heartbreak, so that I may come out whole and cleansed again. For on the other side of my sorrow I know life waits for me. I want to laugh again.

**He shall enter into peace:
they shall rest in their
beds, each one walking in
his uprightness.**

—*ISAIAH 57:2*

TIME helps, Lord, but it never quite
blunts the loneliness that loss brings.
Thank you for the peace that is slowly
seeping into my pores, allowing me to live
with the unlivable; to bear the unbearable.
Guide and bless my faltering steps down a
new road. Prop me up when I think I can't
go it alone; prod me when I tarry too long
in lonely self-pity.

Most of all, Kind Healer, thank you for
the gifts of memory and dreams. The one
comforts, the other beckons, both halves of
a healing whole.

He giveth power to the faint; and to them that have no might he increaseth strength.

—ISAIAH 40:29

DEAREST God, my body is slowing, and I am in need of healing. I am scared of illness and of what lies ahead. I ask now for your healing light to shine upon me and favor me with your grace. I ask now for your love. I give myself to you, God, and I pray that you will help me and heal me. Amen.

**We know that
all things work
together for good to
them that love God,
to them who are
the called according
to his purpose.**

—*ROMANS 8:28*

LORD, only you can comfort us when we grieve. The heaviness we feel at such times can make even breathing a struggle. But you, O Lord, stay close. You fill us with your peace and your comfort. You never let us retreat completely from your light into the darkness of despair. And finally, in your time, you restore joy to our souls. We are ever so grateful, O Great Comforter.

> 66

My grace is sufficient for thee: for my strength is made perfect in weakness. Most gladly therefore will I rather glory in my infirmities, that the power of Christ may rest upon me.

—*2 CORINTHIANS 12:9*

I recently changed jobs. For many years, I'd worked in a doctor's office. During that time, I enjoyed flexible hours, a Godsend when my elderly mother grew ill, but my boss was never supportive and the pay was not ideal. When my mom passed away last year, I decided to look for a different position. I am excited about this next chapter, but change can also be hard.

Dear God, please live in my heart and help me to remain steadfast as I seek to learn, grow, and improve my situation and myself. Please remind me, on the days when my spirit flags, that you are always there.

Therefore whosoever heareth these sayings of mine, and doeth them, I will liken him unto a wise man, which built his house upon a rock.

—*MATTHEW 7:24*

WHEN I am wrong, I turn within to find the right way. God's eternal wisdom is like a flowing river I can tap into at any time, especially when I am clueless and don't know which way to turn. I take comfort in knowing I don't have to be a genius and figure out every last detail of my life. God knows best, and as long as I stay in tune with his Word, I will be divinely inspired.

> **Those things, which ye have both learned, and received, and heard, and seen in me, do: and the God of peace shall be with you.**
>
> —*PHILIPPIANS 4:9*

GOD grant you the joy of learning, as you seek spiritual direction. Listen to those who are wise in the ways of the spirit. Hear the inner workings of your own heart. And grow closer to God.

**Therefore if any
man be in Christ,
he is a new
creature: old things
are passed away;
behold, all things
are become new.**

—2 CORINTHIANS 5:17

CHANGE is inevitable, Lord, we know.
Help us to accept: If we view each
transition as an opportunity to experience
your faithfulness, we make new places in
our lives for spiritual growth.

I will never leave thee, nor forsake thee.

—HEBREWS 13:5

WE are blessed by your enveloping Spirit as near to us as daily changing weather. Your comfort touches us like gentle rain and hushed snow. And, like the sound of thunder and glimpse of searing lightning, you startle us with new opportunities.

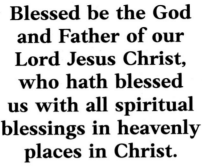

**Blessed be the God
and Father of our
Lord Jesus Christ,
who hath blessed
us with all spiritual
blessings in heavenly
places in Christ.**

—*EPHESIANS 1:3*

THANKSGIVING is almost here, and
Advent and Christmas will follow! Lord,
during this season let me stay focused
on you. Let me be truly thankful for my
blessings, and not so intent on throwing
the perfect party or preparing the best
meal that I forget to be kind to my family
and friends. Thank you for the gifts of
faith, family, and friends!

For where two or three are gathered together in my name, there am I in the midst of them.

—*MATTHEW 18:20*

KEEP us connected, O God of all time, to those who've come before. Inspire us to tell family tales and to pull out family albums and family Bibles and handed-down antiques to show the connecting links of which your love forges us into a collective whole.

Be strong and of a good courage, fear not, nor be afraid of them: for the Lord thy God, he it is that doth go with thee; he will not fail thee, nor forsake thee.

—DEUTERONOMY 31:6

BECAUSE God is good, he loves to bless us, but his deepest longing is for a relationship with us. As you enjoy the good things the heavenly Father has given to you, take time to commune with him, to grow closer to him, and to get to know him a little better.

**Grow in grace, and
in the knowledge of
our Lord and Saviour
Jesus Christ. To him
be glory both now
and for ever. Amen.**

—*2 PETER 3:18*

GROWING in the grace of Christ is to
embrace all that he freely offers me in the
way of love, mercy, and salvation. And
as I grow in his grace, I'll get better and
better at extending love and mercy to
others. To grow in the knowledge of Christ
is to spend time with him in prayer and
worship. As I spend more time with him,
it will get easier and easier to follow the
example he set for us.

A wrathful man stirreth up strife: but he that is slow to anger appeaseth strife.

—PROVERBS 15:18

MY sister Emma and I are like night and day: even though we grew up in the same house, and were raised by the same parents, our worldviews are strikingly different. We've had different ideas about how to help our aging parents, and we have different ideas on how to be a parent. And though we love each other, we don't always get along. Yesterday Emma criticized the way I'm handling a conflict with a mutual friend, and I had to bite my tongue to keep from lashing out. I managed to respond with a joke, and it was amazing, how the tension between us drained away. God, help me to remember: when in a quarrel, I must strive to take the high road. A soft answer can diffuse an argument before it begins.

"

Every idle word that men shall speak, they shall give account thereof in the day of judgment. For by thy words thou shalt be justified, and by thy words thou shalt be condemned.

—*MATTHEW 12:36–37*

BLESS me with the kind heart of a peacemaker and a builder's sturdy hand, Lord, for these are mean-spirited, litigious times when we tear down with words and weapons first and ask questions later. Help me take every opportunity to compliment, praise, and applaud as I rebuild peace.

> ❝
>
> ## If we confess our sins, he is faithful and just to forgive us our sins, and to cleanse us from all unrighteousness.
>
> —*1 JOHN 1:9*

FIRST we have to confess. This is not easy. Pride sometimes gets in the way. It is hard to admit we have done wrong. And sometimes humility gets in the way too. It is hard to feel we are worthy. And indeed we are not.

Fortunately, forgiveness depends on our Father's faithfulness and not our own. And it depends on his justice, since our sins are paid for in Christ. In this way he chooses to forgive. Better yet, he chooses to cleanse our sin, gradually but surely taking away the desires and weaknesses that caused us to fail in the first place. He is willing and able to change those who confess. And he does change them because he is faithful and just.

66

Be merciful unto me, O God, be merciful unto me: for my soul trusteth in thee: yea, in the shadow of thy wings will I make my refuge, until these calamities be overpast. I will cry unto God most high; unto God that performeth all things for me. He shall send from heaven, and save me from the reproach of him that would swallow me up. Selah. God shall send forth his mercy and his truth.

—*PSALM 57:1–3*

ALL we need is God's mercy and truth. In the truth of his promises, we find shelter until any calamity passes and until God rescues us from the accusation of our enemies. In the shadow of his wings, we find mercy, if our soul trusts in him. No matter what trials you face today, cry unto God most high. He will send his mercy and his truth. It's all you need.

How excellent is thy lovingkindness, O God! therefore the children of men put their trust under the shadow of thy wings.

—*PSALM 36:7*

YOU love us Lord, not because we are particularly lovable. And it's certainly not the case that you need to receive our love. I am so heartened by this: You offer your love simply because you delight to do it.

"

For God is not unrighteous to forget your work and labour of love, which ye have shewed toward his name, in that ye have ministered to the saints, and do minister.

—*HEBREWS 6:10*

TODAY, heavenly Father, you may call upon me to listen to someone and hear that person's heart. It may be someone who needs to feel significant enough to be heard, or perhaps someone who is lonely and longs to be connected to another person, or maybe someone who is hurting and needs a sympathetic ear. Whatever the case, Lord, please open my ears so I may listen to someone today. Amen.

NOVEMBER 25

Bear ye one another's burdens, and so fulfil the law of Christ.

—GALATIANS 6:2

LET me not turn away from the oppressed, the needy, Lord, in order to "protect" the children. Instead, nudge me to enlist them with the invitation to help find solutions that we can do as a family. In this way they learn that they, too, can make a difference.

66

When thou makest a feast, call the poor, the maimed, the lame, the blind: And thou shalt be blessed; for they cannot recompense thee: for thou shalt be recompensed at the resurrection of the just.

—*LUKE 14:13–14*

SOME people cannot pay us back for kindnesses we show. And it is these people Jesus says we should invite to dinner. In this story he is at a banquet. He notices a lot of people want the best seats. We should not even want the best seat, he says. And perhaps we should not even invite the "best" people. Humility and service will be rewarded, he teaches. These attitudes are at the heart of his instruction to love our neighbors. And yes, "thou shalt be recompensed," he promises. But not in this life. And not by the people we serve with humility and grace.

**Go thy way, eat thy
bread with joy, and
drink thy wine with
a merry heart; for
God now accepteth
thy works.**

—*ECCLESIASTES 9:7*

BLESS this food. And let it remind us once
again that the soul, like the body, lives and
grows by everything it feeds upon. Keep
us drinking only the good and the pure,
for your glory. Amen.

**Two are better than
one; because they
have a good reward
for their labour.**

—*ECCLESIASTES 4:9*

BLESS my family, Lord. They are a gift
from you, evidence of your unwillingness
for me to be alone. Until I see you face to
face, may the faces of those I love be to
me as your own.

Into whatsoever house ye enter, first say, Peace be to this house.

—LUKE 10:5

LET your peace rest upon our home, dear God. We do not know how to love one another as you have loved us. We fail to reach out the way you have gathered us in. We forget how to give when only taking fills our minds. And, most of all, we need your presence to know we are more than just parents and children. We are always your beloved sons and daughters here. Let your peace rest upon our home, dear God.

Mercy unto you, and peace, and love, be multiplied.
—*JUDE 1:2*

O God the Father, origin of divinity, good beyond all that is good, fair beyond all that is fair, in whom is calmness, peace, and concord; do thou make up the dissensions which divide us from each other, and bring us back into a unity of love, which may bear some likeness to thy divine nature. And as thou art above all things, make us one by the unanimity of a good mind, that through the embrace of charity and the bonds of affection, we may be spiritually one, as well in ourselves as in each other; through that peace of thine which maketh all things peaceful, and through the grace, mercy, and tenderness of thy Son, Jesus Christ. Amen.
—9th-century prayer

WALK WITH GOD

DECEMBER

Behold, I will send my messenger, and he shall prepare the way before me: and the Lord, whom ye seek, shall suddenly come to his temple, even the messenger of the covenant, whom ye delight in: behold, he shall come, saith the Lord of hosts.

—*MALACHI 3:1*

THIS is a prophecy and a promise. It is two promises, actually: one that John the Baptist would come to prepare the way for Jesus, and one that the Lord himself would come in the person of Jesus. Jesus is the one we have sought, the messenger of promise. As you prepare to celebrate his coming at Christmas, delight in him. Behold, he has come.

**Thus saith the Lord,
In an acceptable time
have I heard thee, and
in a day of salvation
have I helped thee: and
I will preserve thee,
and give thee for a
covenant of the people,
to establish the earth.**

—*ISAIAH 49:8*

GOD is not speaking to us in this prophetic text. He is talking to Jesus, long before Jesus was even born. What he is saying is that Jesus would come in an acceptable time, a perfect time, and that the Father would help him and preserve him and gave him a covenant, a promise to give his people. It is nice to know that God is with us. It is nicer to know that he and his Son always had a plan to save us and preserve us.

66

**We have known and
believed the love
that God hath to us.
God is love; and he
that dwelleth in love
dwelleth in God,
and God in him.**

—*1 JOHN 4:16*

I know yours is a persistent devotion, Lord. Your devoted love for me is the example that helps me to love others as well. What would I prefer to your love? What could I love more than those I hold dear? Nothing in the universe! Who are the loves of my life? Let me count them all and delight in them today.

**I bow my knees unto
the Father of our
Lord Jesus Christ,
Of whom the whole
family in heaven and
earth is named.**

—*EPHESIANS 3:14–15*

SOURCE of all life and love, let this family
be a place of warmth on a cold night, a
friendly haven for the lonely stranger,
a small sanctuary of peace in the midst
of swirling activity. Above all, let its
members seek to reflect the kindness of
your own heart, day by day.

> **For thou, Lord, art good, and ready to forgive; and plenteous in mercy unto all them that call upon thee.**
> —*PSALM 86:5*

DEAR God,
Help me forgive my children for their mistakes, and understand that they are small and not yet mature in their behaviors. They don't misbehave because they are bad, but because they are children, and I ask that you always remind me that anything they break or mess up is not as important as making sure they know I love them. Please give me the patience to deal with them when they are bad, and the wisdom to let go of things that are truly not that important, even if I am angry or disappointed. Remind me, God, that I won't have my precious little ones forever, and to cherish and enjoy them while I can. Amen.

Honour thy father and thy mother: that thy days may be long upon the land which the Lord thy God giveth thee.

—*EXODUS 20:12*

ONE of the Ten Commandments, this one includes a promise. If you honor God's purpose by learning from and respecting your parents, you will have the tools for living a long and fruitful life. You can even learn from their negative example if necessary. Respect what God is doing—the land, or place, he put you. And respect your parents too. Honor them and God will honor you.

**Say not thou, What
is the cause that the
former days were better
than these? for thou
dost not enquire wisely
concerning this.**

—*ECCLESIASTES 7:10*

DEAR Father, we wonder why the
pleasures of the past have left us. It
is difficult to realize that they will be
replaced by other pleasures. Please help
us to trust in you as you reconstruct our
lives. Amen.

He is wise in heart, and mighty in strength: who hath hardened himself against him, and hath prospered?

—JOB 9:4

MAY you know that a wisdom and a love transcend the things you will see and touch today. Walk in this light each step of the way. Never forget that there is more to this existence than the material side of things. And be blessed when you suddenly become aware of it: in the smile of a child, in the recognition of your own soul's existence, in the dread of death, and in the longing for immortality.

When pride cometh, then cometh shame: but with the lowly is wisdom.
—*PROVERBS 11:2*

THIS world is full of people who have to be right, even if it means losing friendships or family connections. The need to be right causes so much suffering. Instead, seek the need to be wise. Seek the ability to use your God-given wisdom to be of help to others, and not a burden. No one is right all the time, and it takes wisdom to realize that and to learn to be compassionate to others, and to yourself.

66

**If any man among you
seem to be religious,
and bridleth not his
tongue, but deceiveth
his own heart, this
man's religion is vain.**

—*JAMES 1:26*

AS parties for Christmas and New Year's ramp up, please help me refrain from gossip. Seeing people I haven't seen for a while, I find that the line between catching up and gossiping can be a fine one. It's a temporary pleasure that makes things easier in the moment, seemingly bringing me closer to the people with whom I'm speaking, but it's corrosive over the long term.

> 66

**For I know him, that
he will command
his children and his
household after him,
and they shall keep the
way of the Lord, to do
justice and judgment.**

—*GENESIS 18:19*

LORD, look down upon my family with merciful eyes, and help us to heal the divides that threaten to grow between us. Guide us toward the solutions that will empower everyone involved, and remind us that we work better when we work together. Help us to speak honestly with each other. Amen.

If my people, which are called by my name, shall humble themselves, and pray, and seek my face, and turn from their wicked ways; then will I hear from heaven, and will forgive their sin, and will heal their land.

—*2 CHRONICLES 7:14*

COMING together in worship with prayer, song, and psalm makes us expectant people. Here we find what we came seeking: your abiding, ever-present daily love. We leave, blessed with the truth that it goes with us into the rest of our lives.

**Knowing that a man
is not justified by
the works of the law,
but by the faith of
Jesus Christ, even we
have believed in Jesus
Christ, that we might
be justified by the
faith of Christ, and not
by the works of the
law: for by the works
of the law shall no
flesh be justified.**

—*GALATIANS 2:16*

OUR Father, remind us that to live a life of faith is to live always in your presence, at peace in the home of your love. Amen.

66

Wherefore do ye spend money for that which is not bread? and your labour for that which satisfieth not? hearken diligently unto me, and eat ye that which is good, and let your soul delight itself in fatness. Incline your ear, and come unto me: hear, and your soul shall live; and I will make an everlasting covenant with you, even the sure mercies of David.

—*ISAIAH 55:2–3*

IN this holiday season we may be spending time and money on temporary things which do not really satisfy our hunger or our heart. But there is better food and greater joy than what the world offers. There is spiritual food that is delightful and good. So, listen to God's Word and live, resting in his promises and mercy. They are everlasting and real.

As every man hath received the gift, even so minister the same one to another, as good stewards of the manifold grace of God.

—*1 PETER 4:10*

IT is easier to serve others when my own life is going well. During those chapters in life when things are more or less on an even keel, I am filled with cheer, and I go out into the world wanting to share that goodwill. The act of service comes less easily to me when life presents challenges. When burdened by stress at work, say, or the struggles my son periodically faces from bullies at school, my tendency is to look inward. God, teach me to strive to help others no matter what is going on in my life. You serve us regardless of externals. Service is a gift from you! Remembering this puts me in the right frame of mind to serve others.

DECEMBER 16

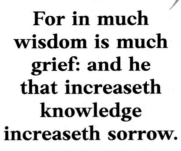

> **For in much wisdom is much grief: and he that increaseth knowledge increaseth sorrow.**
>
> —*ECCLESIASTES 1:18*

THOUGH we may not think there is something to gain in the depths of despair, it is only when we begin to heal that we finally see the truth.

"

Not rendering evil for evil, or railing for railing: but contrariwise blessing; knowing that ye are thereunto called, that ye should inherit a blessing. For he that will love life, and see good days, let him refrain his tongue from evil, and his lips that they speak no guile: Let him eschew evil, and do good; let him seek peace, and ensue it.

—1 PETER 3:9–11

ABIDE in peace, knowing that this is not the first time such trouble has entered the human race. And it is not the kind of crisis that makes a difference to life and death. It will not shed blood or cause great suffering. Yes, it is a problem—with the one, primary quality that characterizes all such tribulations: They all, eventually, come to an end.

**Finally, brethren,
farewell. Be perfect,
be of good comfort,
be of one mind, live
in peace; and the God
of love and peace
shall be with you.**

—2 CORINTHIANS 13:11

IT is good, dear God, to be a part of this family: circle of love, place of rest, bastion of peace. When every other source of comfort fails, this is where I return. Thank you for being in our midst.

I will not leave you comfortless: I will come to you.

—JOHN 14:18

I ask your blessings today on those who may feel alone and lonely: the ill, the housebound, those in nursing homes, the newly divorced. I ask that they feel a sense of your consoling presence. I ask that those who interact with them be moved with a spirit of kindness. Please instill in me that same spirit of kindness, that I will recognize loneliness and be willing to walk with those who are experiencing it!

He that oppresseth the poor reproacheth his Maker: but he that honoureth him hath mercy on the poor.

—*PROVERBS 14:31*

AS the days grow colder and darker, I ask your blessing on those who suffer from the cold: the homeless, those whose furnace went out at the worst time, those who are struggling to pay the heating bill. Please keep them safe, and please motivate the rest of us to help in some way.

Jesus Christ the same yesterday, and to day, and for ever.

—*HEBREWS 13:8*

WE know you, Lord, in the changing seasons: in leaves blazing gently in fall beauty; in winter's snow sculptures. We know you in arid desert cactus bloom and in migration of whale and spawn of fish and turtle. In the blending of the seasons, we feel your renewing, steadfast care, and worries lose their power to overwhelm. The list of your hope-filled marvels is endless, our gratitude equally so.

DECEMBER 22

**If thou draw out
thy soul to the
hungry, and satisfy
the afflicted soul;
then shall thy light
rise in obscurity,
and thy darkness
be as the noon day.**

—*ISAIAH 58:10*

TO extend your soul to the hungry is
to extend to them that which sustains
your own soul. And our soul is sustained
by actual food and drink. The heart of
Christian charity is practical and concrete.

> For the poor shall never cease out of the land: therefore I command thee, saying, Thou shalt open thine hand wide unto thy brother, to thy poor, and to thy needy, in thy land.
>
> —*DEUTERONOMY 15:11*

REMIND us, Lord, that you dwell among the lowliest of people. You are the God of the poor, walking with beggars, making your home with the sick and the unemployed. Keep us mindful always that no matter how much we have, our great calling is to depend on you—for everything, every day of our lives.

66

For unto us a child is born, unto us a son is given: and the government shall be upon his shoulder: and his name shall be called Wonderful, Counsellor, The mighty God, The everlasting Father, The Prince of Peace.

—*ISAIAH 9:6*

ALMIGHTY God, how blessed we are that when you chose to send your son to this earth it was not as the prince of power and domination, but as the Prince of Peace. You knew we would need his peace both as nations populating the earth together and in the innermost places of our hearts. Hear our voices lifted up in gratitude, O God! We are a people who could not survive without the Prince of Peace in our lives. Thank you for your indescribable gift.

66

Suddenly there was with the angel a multitude of the heavenly host praising God, and saying, Glory to God in the highest, and on earth peace, good will toward men.

—*LUKE 2:13–14*

ONE promise of Christmas is the promise of peace. It is what the angels proclaimed to the shepherds: peace on earth and goodwill to all. This is what God has always desired for us, peace for us and between God and man. And this is what he has promised. Don't turn from that. Hear his Word and believe it. That's where true peace is found.

**Blessed are the
pure in heart:
for they shall
see God.**

—*MATTHEW 5:8*

O sovereign and almighty Lord, bless all
thy people, and all thy flock. Give thy
peace, thy help, thy love unto us thy
servants, the sheep of thy fold, that we
may be united in the bond of peace and
love, one body and one spirit, in one hope
of our calling, in thy divine and boundless
love.

—Early Christian Prayer,
The Liturgy of St. Mark

> ❝
> **My little children, let us not love in word, neither in tongue; but in deed and in truth.**
> —*1 JOHN 3:18*

DELIVERER of Peace, you sent Christ to us not as a warrior, not as a judge, not as an enforcer, but as a baby, a healer, a teacher. Help me to follow Christ's example as peacekeeper in my home. Help me instill in my children the ways of peace by acting peaceful not punishing, problem-solving not judging, cooperating not coercing. Help me to show my children your peace so that they may bring peace to others.

66

Thanks be unto God for his unspeakable gift.

—*2 CORINTHIANS 9:15*

THE "season of giving" has just passed, but in your love, Lord, the gifts just keep flowing into my life moment by moment. The new day, the wonders of the season, all the things I take for granted, such as breathing, sipping a mug of hot tea, or enjoying a warm shower—each is a gift from your goodness. As I reflect on your generosity, I'm deeply appreciative for all you've given me.

66

**The kindness and love of
God our Saviour toward man
appeared, Not by works of
righteousness which we have
done, but according to his mercy
he saved us, by the washing of
regeneration, and renewing of
the Holy Ghost; Which he shed
on us abundantly through Jesus
Christ our Saviour; That being
justified by his grace, we should
be made heirs according to the
hope of eternal life.**

—*TITUS 3:4–7*

FATHER, help us to touch and influence
others. We want them to recognize and
celebrate even the small blessings. We
want to surprise them with gestures of
love. Amen.

Blessed are the poor in spirit: for theirs is the kingdom of heaven.

—*MATTHEW 5:3*

GOD, it's so hard to see your will in suffering. But while I can't understand your ways, I trust your heart. And so I cling to the faith that has sustained me through so many heartaches before, knowing that although it may be all I have, it's also all I need. Amen.

> **"**
>
> **In the last days it shall come to pass, that the mountain of the house of the Lord shall be established in the top of the mountains, and it shall be exalted above the hills; and people shall flow unto it.**
>
> —*MICAH 4:1*

ON a bad day, it's nice to know how the story ends. If empires crumble or disaster strikes, God's people look forward to the day when the house of the Lord shall be established. His temple will be restored and lifted up, as people from every nation flow into it, praising and worshiping him. The whole earth will be filled with peace and prosperity and justice. And the glory of the Lord will be seen by all.